UNDER
THE WING
OF A PATRIOT

UNDER THE WING OF A PATRIOT

THE LIFE STORY OF USAF FIGHTER PILOT COL. JIM RYAN

SHANE ALLEN

TATE PUBLISHING
AND ENTERPRISES, LLC

Published by Tate Publishing & Enterprises, LLC
127 E. Trade Center Terrace | Mustang, Oklahoma 73064 USA
1.888.361.9473 | www.tatepublishing.com

Tate Publishing is committed to excellence in the publishing industry. The company reflects the philosophy established by the founders, based on Psalm 68:11,
"The Lord gave the word and great was the company of those who published it."

Book design copyright © 2014 by Tate Publishing, LLC. All rights reserved.
Cover design by Rodrigo Adolfo
Interior design by Caypeeline Casas

Published in the United States of America

ISBN: 978-1-63306-197-2
Biography & Autobiography / Military
14.11.04

To Jim's late wife, Jeanie Ryan, who stood
by his side for sixty strong years.

Bethlyn Jean 'Nana' Ryan
November 11, 1931–April 24, 2014.

Colonel Jim Ryan as base commander at
Cannon AFB in Clovis, New Mexico.

ACKNOWLEDGMENTS

This book is dedicated to all the great pilots I had the pleasure of flying with, including those in the 401st and 355th Tactical Fighter Wings.

For my loving family, thank you for all the care and support through the years. I know I caused you worry, and for that, I'm truly sorry, but I couldn't have done it without you.

To all my friends, I hope you enjoy reading this book about my life as much as I enjoyed living it.

Lastly, a special thank you to my Lord. I know I never flew alone.

Col. Jim Ryan

CONTENTS

FOREWORD

You are at the leading edge of a story about a USAF fighter pilot. Jim Ryan is a friend, and I can say I admire him for how he flew and led others in the business of tactical air operations in peace and at war.

The fact that he was a forward air control (FAC) pilot during combat operations in Vietnam attests to his remarkable skills and courage in flying close to the ground at low speeds while directing tactical fighter pilots where to aim their loads of bombs, napalm, and rockets, as well as strafing with guns in direct support of ground forces. Enjoy this ride about a real professional.

Tucson, Arizona
Bill Hosmer
USAF Pilot (Retired)

LETTER

June 8, 2013

Dear Jim,

Upon starting to write, I realized our service together was over forty years ago, and many years have dimmed my memory. So I did write of what could be remembered, and I'll be glad to take calls from your author.

It takes one to know one—this old cliché is certainly applicable to the business of fighter aircraft employment.

I was inducted into the US Army Air Corps on February 4, 1943. Upon getting my wings, I served as a fighter pilot in WWII, Korea, Vietnam, and several police actions. I flew P-40s, T-33s, F-86Fs, F-86Ds, F-100s, F-104s and F-4 Phantom IIs, as well as 0-1 Bird Dogs. I know a fighter pilot when I fly with one. James "Fuzz" Ryan was a fighter pilot, one of the best who ever pushed a throttle.

In the early 1960s, the United States sold Germany a fleet of F-104 aircraft. The US Air Force was required to train German pilots to fly the bird. This was done at Luke AFB in Arizona. I arrived there in June 1964 to participate in the program. Because international relations were a consideration, the air force hand-picked top-notch fighter pilots for the job. Fuzz Ryan was one of them, and we flew together at Luke AFB for two years. It was plain to me that Fuzz was top notch among some of the best fighter pilots in the world.

In the summer of 1966, Ryan and I were assigned to Vietnam, though not in the same shipment. We were both tabbed to be forward air controllers because of much experience and expertise in the fighter usage. Though in different outfits, we worked closely in the same geographical area and saw each other often.

Once when we landed at the same airstrip, Jim was flying an army helicopter. He flew anything that had the capability to get off the ground.

At one time, in the fall of 1966, it seemed that the enemy was trying to move a lot of their troops through our area, traveling south. We stayed busy controlling air strikes. Jim, while withering enemy fire, put his 90 mph 0-1 directly over the enemy in order to mark their position with white phosphorus rockets, which assisted much in helping neutralize enemy forces.

For his valor in aerial combat, I submitted him for a Silver Star. This award is third in prestige behind the Medal of Honor and the Air Force Cross. Unfortunately, I never learned if he received this decoration.

From Vietnam, we both were assigned to the East Coast area of the Continental United States—me at Tactical Air Command Headquarters located at Norfolk, Virginia, and Jim at USAF Command Headquarters at the Pentagon, Washington DC. We managed a couple of small-game hunting trips to southwest Virginia where I still reside. We mostly hunted ruffled grouse, which is the toughest shot gunning in the world. When grouse flush, they have an uncanny ability to get a tree between them and the shooter. If no big trees are handy, they get behind the thickest brush, not to be seen. I remember two shots Jim made. He got one grouse and missed one. His other shots I didn't see, but a 50 percent kill ratio is out of this world. As an old grouse hunter, I am tickled if I get one out of three.

Every military pilot is a good pilot. He can fly a passenger plane holding 4 to 350 passengers, a cargo plane, a refueling tanker, or a bomber. On planes with lots of motors, there is a pilot, a copilot, and a navigator, and on bombers, a bombardier and gunners to make up an aircrew. On most fighters, there is only one man. He's pilot, copilot, navigator, bombardier, and gunner, making up the aircrew. This helps us understand why it takes several years to make a fighter pilot out of a pilot.

In Vietnam, we ran short of fighter pilots because for one, the brainpower in DC had not programmed enough, and two, they took over 2,000 of us professional fighter jocks for forward air control duty—338 of which were killed in action.

To take up the slack, the DC brainpower sent passenger, cargo, tanker, and various other pilots to a ninety-day fighter indoctrination program and then shipped them to Vietnam. They didn't know what they were doing and knew they didn't know. Their attitude ranged from frustrated to bitter.

About one-third of the fighters I got for a strike were these guys. After I risked my neck flying over the bad guys in a 0-1 to mark their exact location with a Willie Pete (white phosphorous) rocket, these guys dropped their ordinance, maybe five hundred yards away so as to avoid flying over the enemy and getting shot at. It was obvious that their primary objective was not to help win the war, but to survive their tour. This weighed heavily on others and me.

About one-third of the time, I got navy fighters not afraid to get in there and mix it with the Charlies (enemy), though their accuracy was not quite as good as USAF.

The other third of the time I got air force professionals. This gave me a good feeling because I knew we were going to put a big hurt on the bad guys.

B.B. Huffman, US Fighter Pilot
New Castle, Virginia

THE MAKINGS

Born in the height of the Great Depression, Jim Ryan expected hardship, but desire and faith overshadowed any feeling of doubt or uncertainty for his future. In fact, his humble beginnings did nothing but make him stronger. He never owned a bicycle or complained of walking; money was scarce, but there was always food on the table. His family was tight in every way, their bond outweighed material things and money didn't matter.

His father, Ernest Ryan, was part Cherokee-Choctaw Indian, and he worked hard to provide for his family by logging, farming, and mining while his mother not only maintained the household, she also did her share in other ways. She wasn't afraid of running a plow behind a mule or climbing up a six-hundred-foot ladder to a small hut atop a smoke tower at the Phelps Dodge copper-smelting plant near Planetside, Arizona. It was a job most men avoided.

The couple raised most of their own food and taught five-year-old Jim and his sister, just two years younger, the way of the land in Lodi, Oklahoma. Ernest, with five brothers in other areas of the United States, never passed an opportunity for a better living by moving outside impoverished Lodi. The first of many moves was to Arizona for the copper mine boom, then to Kansas for wheat farming, dairy, and ultimately, oil-field work. Despite traveling from one state to the next, Jim still calls Lodi his home place since it was where he spent most of his childhood cutting his teeth.

Lodi, a small community—even smaller today, with no recent census report—sits quaintly in the Sans Bois Mountains of southeast Oklahoma, where buffalo roamed free among Indian settlers who occupied the Indian Territory through 1907. Jim was born there in 1932, only twenty-five years after Oklahoma became a state. With no doctor nearby, he was delivered by midwives inside his parents' home, which stood strongly on a wooden foundation about one mile north of a little schoolhouse crafted with colorful stone from the surrounding mountains. The pristine countryside was one from a storybook for a young child to grow up. Other than the school, the only other mark of civilization was a post office attached to a general store stocked with common supplies made available to the fewer than fifty people living in the tiny community. With little commerce and no real economy, only natives made this place home by surviving on self-sufficiency; there was no other way.

Jim became perfectly content with a life that would be considered poor by most. "When I had the choice to go to the store and spend a nickel on candy or the mountains, I chose the mountains, where there was always more to eat," he said. Jim and his sister, Ernestine, had every hickory nut, black walnut tree, huckleberry bush, wild grapevine, and wild plum thicket fixed in memory. Clear rocky streams fed naturally by groundwater were absolutely full of largemouth bass, perch, and catfish. White-tailed deer populated the thick pine forests, leaving tracks all over the rich soil. Hunting game and butchering farm-raised hogs kept the smokehouses full, filling the air with the scent of cured meat. Jim began the life of a plainsman as a child, with a slingshot handy if by chance he spotted a squirrel to lend to the family's food supply.

"My mom and dad were busy working and trusted my ability early on, so they didn't worry about me as long as I was home for dinner," recounts Jim. His parents worked hard for the little money they earned, so he made a point not to take from them if possible. He kept busy by catching wild pigs or rattling possums and coons out of trees for their skins. Animal pelts were a source of income, and the fur was plentiful for the taking, so he did what he could by selling the hides to buyers who made frequent stops through the area.

Outdoorsmen keep like company, and Swamp and Cottontail Brooks were close in age, with common interests and energy. They lived near Jim. The Brooks brothers were named after types of rabbits and, like rabbits, were quick on their feet, always only steps behind Jim. Like wingmen in formation, they went where he did, always knowing it would be a worthwhile adventure following his lead.

Jim remembers vividly a warm summer day in May, after school was out for break. He and the Brooks brothers were anxious to break away from the books to put their attention on the natural playground that awaited them. Jim asked if they were up for some fishing. Swamp and Cottontail were boys of few words, quickly replying, "Yep." What the brothers lacked in sophistication, they made up for with aptitude in catching fish. Jim overlooked their hillbilly nature for their stronger qualities, like their ambition to live on the land, which required no savoir faire. Although more refined himself, he understood their ways, never showing any discrimination. Even though they were different, they were friends.

Jim's mother, Faye, was the daughter of a Phillips 66 oilman, a widower. After losing her mother early in life to illness, it was just the two of them, and his busy schedule called for the help of servants, who cared for Faye while he was away on business. She was well-educated and taught proper—something she passed on to Jim and Ernestine. Refinement and worldly wisdom was insisted and learned despite their simple surroundings.

Bear Creek was a popular fishing destination marked by the fifteen-foot, twenty-foot, and thirty-foot holes—all reference points for places to meet. The fifteen-foot hole was well-known from miles around as the best place to swim. It was a magnet destination for locals and out-of-town people to take advantage of its clean clear water. The banks were grassy, and there was a leaning oak tree in perfect position to dive from, which brought people from miles around to picnic during the summer. Jim asked Swamp and Cotton to meet him at the fifteen-foot hole with their gear in one hour, and the boys obliged with another yep. They met at the hole where the water was so clear that you could nearly see the bottom. Unable to pass up the opportunity, they stripped their clothes off for a swim before setting out on their trip. After an hour, they dried off their bodies with the same clothes they were wearing, then put only their pants back on, forgoing their shoes and shirt. Lessening their load, they left those there to pick up when passing back through later.

As daylight progressed, so did they, making their way farther down Bear Creek through the winding valleys of the mountains. The boys moved through the waist-deep water with strings of catfish and perch secured to their belt loops, weighing them down. As the sun dragged behind the mountaintops, they moved forward. The fish were biting, and they couldn't stop. Their sunburned noses ached but started to feel better from the oncoming shade; they were lost in time. Now farther down Bear Creek than times past, they had never caught so many fish; no one wanted it to end.

Wading through the water, Jim kept pulling his stringer up to take a look at his catch. The reason being, he wanted to make sure there was no water moccasin latched to the fish, like a time before when he'd been surprised to find seven snakes clamped to a catch he was dragging, one he'd had to cut loose quickly.

Snakes were prevalent in the cool water this time of year, and if bit, they would be too far from home to survive. The water snakes referred to as (cottonmouth) water moccasins got large and venomous enough to kill a grown man, much less a child, with one strike. They were good swimmers, like slow-moving water, and preyed on fish, making the boys an easy target.

Cottontail and Swamp dragged their stringers up too for frequent inspection. They would look over at Jim and nod before dropping their line back in the water. Jim looked at them with a grin and simply nodded back. The Brooks boys liked his approval. He was their confidant, and they respected him.

With the sun now completely out of sight behind the mountains, Jim suddenly realized with panic that they were too far from home to make it back on time. With more words than had been shared all day, Jim said with distress, "Guys, we need to get back home quick. We're going to be late, and I've never been late getting home."

With no hesitation, they pulled their stringers up and took to the sandy creek bank, where the ground was packed well for running. In a hurry, they followed it as far as they could. Then they climbed up the sloping bankside to a beat-up cattle trail, safe from stickers in their feet. The frugal Lodi cattle owners turned their stock loose in the mountains to graze, which saved them money on feed. Herds of cattle roamed the mountains, chewing on little bluestem and Indian grass and excavating clear paths with their hooves. The boys hustled down the trail, careful not to step in a fresh cow paddy along the way.

When they got to the fifteen-foot hole, they quickly stopped for their shirts and shoes. They made better time with their shoes on, not having to worry about stickers since the cow trail ended.

They finally arrived at the bridge that was the close mile marker to each of their houses in opposite directions. The boys said good night then wished each other good luck for the trouble they all risked. Swamp and Cottontail weren't too worried since they had been this late getting home before, with little said by their parents, but Jim on the other hand was anxiety-ridden beyond his wits. The last mile, he rehearsed what he was going to say to his dad, who trusted him to be back home before dark.

It wasn't so much the punishment but, more so, the disappointment he had in himself for losing track of time. He and his parents shared respect, and Jim knew that being late was unacceptable. It was something out of character for him, something he hadn't done to them before. Earlier that day, his mother had asked that he be careful of the snakes. She was probably in the floor crying by now. He began to think the worst. His dad could already be on his way out to look for them. Precariously panting, Jim came through the clearing where his house sat. He could see a kerosene lamp glowing from the distance on his front porch, and next to it was the silhouette of a large man sitting in a chair.

Jim slowed to a walk about thirty yards away and then he saw his father stand up to make his way down the steps of the porch.

Jim met him with the stringer of fish in hand, which were now ruined from the distance he had to travel. He never considered dropping them because he thought they might serve as a token of reasoning for why he wasn't on time. His father grabbed Jim's ten-year-old arm more firmly than ever before and asked in an adamant voice, "Where have you been?" Jim dropped the fish to the ground.

His mother stepped outside, and Jim saw her glistening tear-stained cheeks from the glow of the lantern. She said, "Thank God you're okay." His heart got very heavy, and he was at a loss for words.

Ernest quickly told Faye to go back inside, and Jim knew he was in trouble, more than ever before. He trembled when he noticed his dad taking the belt from his waist, one hand still gripping his arm tightly.

In an instant, he was facedown on the ground. Then he felt the sting on his rear end being busted with the strapping leather. Young Jim tried holding back any emotion, yet there was no stopping it.

Ernest helped him up from the ground and wiped the gritty tears from his cheeks with his thumb.

Young Jim looked his dad in the eyes, fighting off the emotion with all his might, knowing men didn't cry. Then he saw his dad wiping his own tears.

He and his father sat on the edge of the porch crying together. Arms tightly around each other's necks, side by side, they wept. Sharing a feeling that only a boy and father can truly understand, they bonded from the incident. Jim made a vow to never be late again. Ernest hadn't struck his son before that night, and he never did again. Jim never gave him another reason to.

From that point forward, Jim kept close attention to every minute—a strict code that played an important role throughout his future.

Growing older, Jim and his sister finished elementary school in Lodi, and that was the end of the daily two-mile walk to school. Now they had to bus about seven miles away to a small town called Red Oak, where the middle and high school was. They met many new friends because the Red Oak schools served all the surrounding communities. Many of the new friends they made, they're still in contact with today. Those are June and John Fields, along with June's brother Chuck Gallagher and his wife, Nel. "I had great fun with those people. I love them and always will," said Jim, reflecting back.

It was now 1948. America was rebounding from the Depression, and President Harry S. Truman had just been elected in the greatest election upset in American history, defeating conservative Thomas E. Dewey. Truman, who stood for the common man, had set the United States on the road to recovery, putting many back to work. Faye's sister, Inez Banks, had reached out to the family with good news. Her letter spoke of a burgeoning economy spurred by wheat cropping, oil, railroads, and manufacturing.

After moving to Arizona on two separate short stints, the family knew how difficult it was to move and reestablish residency, but this time was different. With WWII at an end, certain parts of the United States were developing. Nearby Kansas stood for American ideals. It was time the Ryan family acted upon their own, so they made the move.

Sixteen-year-old Jim and his sister were about to start high school, but as children from the silent generation, they had little to say about the decision to move. After all, they had heard talk about a different America that involved individualism and pursuing dreams, something that Lodi wasn't offering yet. Television was becoming more visible, and cars were commonplace. By this time Ford had introduced the F-Series pickup, the Lincoln Continental was on the assembly line, and Cadillac added tail fins to the shape of their body style—a progressive trend in the making.

Ernest and Faye purchased an Oldsmobile for the new life they were going to establish in Lyons. Ernest drove the car out first to make arrangements for the family before Faye, Jim, and Ernestine followed. Ernest quickly found a job with Herndon Drilling Company in the oil field and went straight to work. Uncle Banks, who was established and had some time on his hands, made the trip South in his pickup truck to bring the rest of the Ryan family back to their new home in Kansas.

Faye and the kids loaded their possessions, including the family radio that they used to listen to the *Grand Ole Opry* on Friday and Saturday nights, something they enjoyed together as a family. The tall mountains made it difficult to get broadcast signals other than Chicago-based WSN radio's fifty thousand watts, which much of Canada and the United States picked up with ease two nights a week. The kids hoped the move would help the family with new beginnings which could include a TV, but at the least, the flatlands of the Sunflower State would likely bring an expanded variety of radio broadcasts like CBS, ABC, and NBC.

After a near five-hour ride in the back of the pickup, Jim and his sister were happy to see the waving wheat fields of the Midwest. The Bankses' home in McPherson wasn't big enough to accommodate everyone, so Jim was dropped off with his older cousin Kirby, who was working in the oil field eighty miles outside of Lyons. He had his own place, with room for Jim until further plans were made. Jim didn't mind staying with Kirby, twenty years his senior, who liked to hunt and fish during his free time. They did a lot of that between servicing oil wells.

Not much time passed before the Ryan family found a home to rent near the high school in Lyons, and Jim moved in.

Lyons moved at a faster pace than the backwoods of Lodi, which was truly eye-opening for Jim and his sister. The biggest differences were indoor plumbing, which made for a bathroom inside. Wired electricity lit the rooms of their house and eliminated the need for batteries in their radio, which Jim plugged in for the first time to hear the voice of Hank Williams singing "Move It on Over" through the single speaker. He really liked country music, then and now.

It was a short time before high school would start, so he began to familiarize himself with his new surroundings, including a visit to his mom's workplace—the Oldsmobile car dealership in town. Next door was a feed store that caught Jim's attention, so he went there afterward.

When he walked through the front door, someone drew his full attention. She sat behind the counter with the biggest, prettiest smile he had ever seen. She said, "I'm Jeanie. Can I help you find something?"

In his mind, he thought, *I think I just found it*, before using his words to answer, "No thanks, I'm new in town and just looking around." She smiled again, and he liked it, hoping she wouldn't stop. After looking around the store, he said good-bye to Jeanie, still smiling. Jim said, "Maybe I'll see you at school?" She thought to herself, *I hope so*, then answered with one word, "Maybe."

School started, and Jim excelled in academics. As a distance runner, he ran varsity track. He did see Jeanie at school, but with her being a year behind him, it was not as often as he hoped.

His senior year came and went. After graduation, he took a job with Herndon Drilling Company as a swamper on a roustabout truck as part of the crew that moved drilling rigs from location to location. He worked not only in Kansas but Colorado and Nebraska as well. The work was hard and not exactly what he had in mind long-term. Temperatures from hot to extremely cold were always a problem, and he remembers all those numerous times they had weather well below zero. He wasn't a fan of the cold, but he managed what turned out to be one last winter on the job.

It was a late fall afternoon when he finished his workday and then headed to his parents' house, where he was staying while saving money. On his way home, he was thinking of how he might find something else to do before another winter.

Arriving home, he walked through the door to head for the shower, but suddenly, he noticed an infectious smile he hadn't seen in a while, and there was no mistaking who it belonged to. His sister had a friend over that evening which, to his surprise, was Jeanie, who was sitting in his living room. She was older now, and even prettier than when they first met.

He asked her out that night, and she said yes, suggesting they go to the movies. "I work there and can get us in. There's a new movie you might enjoy called *Air Cadet*. It's about air force fighter pilots, and I feel like you might enjoy it."

It was 1951, and jet fighter pilots were being portrayed in Hollywood with great fame due to constant press of the Korean War, more specifically MiG Alley in North Korea, where the Yalu River empties into the Yellow Sea. This was where numerous dogfights occurred between US F-86 Sabre fighter jets and Soviet MiG-15s. The first American jet aces were born from this conflict, the top three being Joseph McConnell, James Jabara, and Frederick Blesse, in that order and with many more to follow. United States ace status is reached with five confirmed enemy aircraft kills. These top three US aces are still accounted for as having the most air-to-air victories in US military history today.

Jim had heard of these great American flying aces and quickly agreed to the movie. Little did he know, he would later connect with the aforementioned American heroes, and would even fly with Jabara and Blesse. He never flew with McConnell, but he did fly in the movie made about his life titled *The McConnell Story*. It starred Alan Ladd and June Allison and will be discussed in coming chapters.

The McConnell story was made after McConnell's death while testing the fifth production F-86H-1-NA fighter jet, the last version of the F-86 Sabre known for destroying the (Russian) MiG-15 fighters at a ratio of fifteen to one during the Korean War. The F-86H was the forerunner to the F-100D, which was famously utilized by all USAF fighter units throughout the mid-1950s and '60s. It was during a time the American flying aces were respected by the world.

INSPIRED

It was Saturday night when Jim and Jeanie strolled under the brightly lit marquee sign displaying that *Air Cadet* was now showing. They made their way through the crowd of teenagers in front of the theater who were waiting for the ticket office to open. Jeanie, as a part-time employee, earned the privilege of walking straight through with no wait.

After stopping at the concession for popcorn and soft drinks, they entered the room, sitting directly center midway—the best seats in the house—before the crowd meandered through the tight aisles for showtime. The lights dimmed, and the 8-millimeter film rolled. Crackling audio filled the room with a thunderous jet roar from a T-33 (training jet) soaring across the silver screen. Suddenly, sound of a man's voice echoed, "You too can do this." It was the opening of a United States Air Force recruiting commercial that aired before the movie began. Jim captivated by the imagery, quickly cut his eyes toward Jeanie, who was comfortably seated next to him. She had never witnessed him so engaged, as if it was him in the cockpit of the T-33.

The movie was about a group of cadets going through air force pilot training during the Korean War and eventually moving on to the advanced fighter jet program, where one of them falls in love with the wife of an instructor, jeopardizing his future as a fighter pilot. As the drama unfolded, Jim and Jeanie were so close they could have shared a single seat. The film concluded with, "You too can be a United States Air Force fighter pilot. See your nearest recruiting office today."

This message rang through young Jim's head with great impact, as if it was directed to him solely—a calling. When the lights came on, Jeanie noticed the glow in his eyes and quickly realized a fire was lit for great cause. Something large had come over Jim. Without him saying a word, she felt his intense passion. It was the budding of a kindred spirit they would share for a lifetime— a mutual understanding. They left the theater hand in hand, and not only did Jim realize his future, she did too; she would be his devotee. She knew what he was going to say before he said it; it was crystal clear. Jim confirmed with her he wanted to be a fighter pilot. She concurred he would make a great fighter pilot, and there wasn't any reason he shouldn't pursue it. So he did.

Early the next morning, he walked out to the main highway and, with his feet hugging the edge of the pavement, put his thumb in the air to catch a ride to the air force recruiting station thirty-five miles away in Hutchison, Kansas. In a few minutes, a truck spotted him and pulled over to the shoulder of the road, and Jim climbed in. The passerby took him downtown, let him out, and said, "Good Luck."

Jim walked through the door to be greeted by a recruiting officer who asked him to please sit. Without wasting time on small talk, and before the recruiter had a chance to say, "What brings you in?" Jim got straight to the point. He said, "I watched a movie last night called *Air Cadet* and understand that if I can pass all the requirements, I too can become a jet pilot in the United States Air Force?"

With some hesitation, the recruiter said, "That's a possibility, but you don't look very old, certainly not old enough to have passed a college exam?"

Without delay, Jim replied, "I understand there must be requirements asked of me, but there was nothing about needing a college degree in the commercial. If you allow me to meet all requirements outside of having a college degree, giving me something in writing stating such, I'll sign up today to join the air force."

The recruiting officer obliged by explaining he would only have to pass physical, aptitude, and achievement testing. Since he met the age requirement of nineteen years old, there was no reason he couldn't give him the opportunity. He closed by telling Jim there was no guarantee he would make a pilot. It would hinge on his personal determination, discipline, ability, and most importantly, the results from all testing.

Jim enlisted that day. He left with instruction to pack a bag of belongings for basic training and testing at Sampson Air Force Base (AFB) in Geneva, New York. In a week, a car would be sent to pick him up and drop him off at the train station at Wichita, Kansas—the home of a great patriot you'll read about later. Enlistees from the central area like Jim usually went to Lackland AFB in San Antonio, Texas, for basic training, but that base was overflowing at the time Jim enlisted, so he went to New York.

Feeling great satisfaction from the meeting, he left with full confidence, wondering what New York would be like. Somehow, he knew it would be a far cry from Kansas. This was the beginning of the rest of his life starting to show itself; it was an opportunity to make a career in something requiring more than a strong back.

When he made it back home late that night, Jim told his parents and Jeanie he would be leaving in a week for basic training in the air force. It was an exciting but worrying time for everyone with America at war, but with great reward, there were always risks—something they understood. Jim's compassion overshadowed any reason of doubt from anyone.

The following week, at 8:00 a.m. sharp on the morning scheduled, a white Chevy pulled in the driveway of Jim's home as he expected. He was waiting at the door. Jim leaned over, grabbed his bag, and began his good-byes to his family. As he stood up straight, he wiped a tear from his mother's cheek and then promised to send pictures and write when he could. He left her by saying, "Don't worry about me. I'll be fine."

Jim never thought about not being able to pass a test or failing, but rather, he thought about what it was going to feel like to fly a jet plane and what type of life it would bring him. Just as sure, Jeanie hugged him and said, "Just be yourself, and you'll pass with flying colors." As he walked through the door, his dad gave him a pat on the shoulder and said, "Do well, son, and most of all, be careful. I love you."

Reaching the train station, he was handed his papers, including a ticket to board for Geneva, New York, over a day east by rail. Not only had Jim never been close to New York, he had never been on a train. He never expected his first time to experience both would be as an air force enlisted man; he was literally on a fast track.

When he arrived in New York, he was tired from having gotten no sleep on the train, but he thought it would be good conditioning for what was ahead; he always found the positive. Hundreds of men ready to serve their country were in line at the front office to check in for basic military training or boot camp, the first stage in preparing servicemen mentally, physically, and emotionally for the military.

Once training started, he found the rigors of boot camp not much different from his last job in Kansas, so he modestly met the challenge by picking up the slack for others when he could. Near the end of the ninety days required, he began testing for an Air Force Specialty Code (AFSC) to find out what he would be most qualified to do in the air force.

After completion of testing, he was given three choices of jobs—communications, security, or control tower operator. He took the third option because it was a natural step in the right direction, keeping him around and involved with airplanes.

After basic training, Jim was assigned to Keesler AFB in Biloxi, Mississippi, to attend control tower operator school with one thing in mind—the long-term goal.

The first time he stepped foot on an aircraft was in the C-47 that took him to Keesler. When he arrived, he went straight to his commander's office to give him the letter from the recruiter that stated he could test for the Aviation Cadet Pilot Training Program and to find out when that could take place. The commander told him to be patient, aware that there were many students at Keesler who were interested in trying out for the same program. He went on to say that in a few weeks, all those people would be notified of the time and place for testing. There were many others from outside the base who would test there for the program. That was the information Jim was looking for. Self-affirmation made him feel better. The commander continued, "The process will consist of a full week of testing, so you will be excused from tech school for the amount of time that it takes." True to his word, in a couple of weeks, Jim received a written order telling him where and when to report to start the rigorous testing.

When the day came, he realized many others had gotten the same notice. As it turned out, there were more than a thousand others there to test. Trying to get so many students in the assigned building was a challenge, and Jim ended up taking a seat on the floor to test that day. He quickly learned he would need to arrive extremely early to get a desk and chair, which were limited. Testing lasted for five full days, and at the end of each day, test results were posted on a board outside the room. Cuts were made each day, with the names of those who passed being put on the board and expected to return for testing the next day. Those whose names were not posted were asked to return to their tech school the very next day.

Day by day, Jim's name appeared on the board as the crowd dwindled in numbers, making it easy to find a chair and desk. Finally, the last day came on a Friday, and after the test, Jim approached the board to find his name. He had finished the written part.

After the written tests, everybody still remaining were asked to take a flight physical the following Monday. The physical was a comprehensive physical that was beyond thorough. In fact, it took two days to complete, and several did not pass. If you were not physically perfect, you didn't measure up to standards. Jim again met the requirements before reporting back to tech school to await further instruction.

Once back, he waited anxiously for a few weeks before the eighty who had passed the written and physical requirements were transported by bus to Moody AFB in Valdosta, Georgia, to complete the last and final testing of the program.

This part of the testing was the stanine group, which not only evaluated intellect on a speed-of-completion basis but had a heavy emphasis on coordination, dexterity, physical strength, and decision-making ability as well. Stanine was long and demanding, and it lasted for three days and three nights.

When it was over, the students bussed back to Keesler AFB to resume their technical school training. Beat from exhaustion, they all slept on the ride back.

A month passed, and Jim still hadn't heard any feedback, but he remained patient. Then the big day came when he was in the barracks. He was called by name to report to the commander's office as soon as possible. He was in the process of getting ready to head to class and had no idea of what this could be about. Hurrying into the office, he met the commander's secretary at the front desk. She advised him to be seated and wait for the others who were coming. They would all go in together to see the commander. It wasn't long until eight other young men followed suit into the waiting area. After the last arrived, they were asked to go in and report. Walking into the commander's door, they stood at attention. Then each sternly saluted their superior. "Reporting as ordered, sir," they said in unison.

Standing, the commander informed them of the good news. "It's a pleasure to tell you that you nine people have passed all your tests and have now fully qualified for the Aviation Cadet Pilot Training Program. Congratulations to you all. You will now complete your schooling here. Then after graduation, your next assignment base and specialty will be given to you." Once there, each would be told by the Air Training Command Headquarters in Waco, Texas, when and where they start the Aviation Cadet Pilot Training Program.

That was it. Jim was in and on his way. It was the greatest feeling in his entire life; it was a dream come true. To this day, he says, "You can do anything if you want it bad enough." This was a monumental point in his life, a standard he continued to keep.

On a side note, Jim said that after that day, when he stood there for the news with the eight others who made it into the Aviation Cadet Pilot Training Program, he never saw them again. Never knowing anything else about them, he often wonders who they were and where they ended up.

Once he finished control tower operator school in July 1952, he was assigned to Randolph AFB in San Antonio, Texas, to work the control tower while waiting to get more notice on the Aviation Cadet Pilot Program. Before reporting, he asked for leave (vacation) and caught a flight on a B-25 twin-engine plane out of Keesler and flew back to Wichita, Kansas. He couldn't wait to share the news with his family and friends. Dropped off in Wichita, he hitchhiked back to Lyons, where he spent a week with Jeanie and his mother and father, all extremely excited to see him. They were particularly happy to hear his news of making it into the program—what he sat out to do only a short time before.

Jim also had a surprise for Jeanie. By picking up other soldiers' kitchen patrol duties at basic training, he had saved enough money to buy an engagement ring that he presented her with after getting home. She gladly said yes to marriage, but they couldn't marry until he finished the Aviation Cadet Pilot Training Program. It was a clear rule that cadets could not be married or get married until graduating from the year-and-a-half program as commissioned second lieutenants in the USAF.

Getting engaged to be married wasn't all he intended on while home. He also bought a 1950 Chevy coupe, which he drove back to Randolph AFB to report to his job in the control tower after a nice visit. Working the control tower was even more enjoyable now that he knew he was getting closer to flying the aircraft he admired every day. It was a good way to occupy his time before he began training to fly. Back at Randolph, only days before

Christmas, he received a letter stating the first stage of Aviation Cadet Pilot Training (Pre-Flight) would begin on 29 January 1953 at Lackland AFB in San Antonio, Texas. It was all going according to plan.

FLYING

Just a short time ago, Jim had finished high school, still uncertain of his future. Now he was on his way to the Aviation Cadet Pilot Training Program—his first step toward flying the jet fighter aircraft that had soared across the screen in the inspirational movie *Air Cadet*. The small window of opportunity had created sudden urgency, which Jim acted upon without hesitation. It was a simple measure for forward thinkers, who lived within the moment, in tune with one's self and able to identify opportunity and follow through.

When he enlisted in the air force, he was given entry rank of airman basic, bearing no insignia and little pay; it was a start. Three months came to pass, earning him a stripe and $84 per month as airman third class. After receiving notice to report to pilot training, he was immediately bumped to the pay grade of staff sergeant and given a nice raise. Jim didn't get to wear the rank, but he was making $154 per month working the control tower, three times what he made less than a year ago.

Not only was he good at his control tower job, but also Randolph AFB, which opened in 1931, was a special place to start. It was considered the showplace of the air force because of the Spanish Colonial revival style architecture. The headquarters building was referred to throughout the air force as the

Taj Mahal, or simply, the Taj. Two control towers stood on the base. An eight-story-high main tower on the east side, used for regular routine day-and-night traffic, was open 24/7. The other two-story tower on the west side was used for training purposes and only opened when needed. Jim vividly recalls operating the west tower one day, when a superior from the other tower noticed nine aircraft in the traffic pattern on his side. The planes were B-29s making touch-and-go landings, a phase of their training performed by new pilots practicing to land then take off again in one turnkey drill.

Jim kept close observation of all the giant planes on his board by marking their position every step of the way, maintaining their spacing to prevent any problems.

This many B-29s in the flight pattern was far beyond normal routine for a trainee. So the superior went over to question Jim. He said, "Why are so many airplanes in the holding pattern and two on final approach together?"

Jim stiffly responded, "I have it under control. There is no use in holding them back any more than I need to. I have a close eye, and communication with them is ongoing."

It made more sense to Jim to keep the flight pattern loaded tight rather than stalling to create unneeded space, which would take more time. The officer questioning him had more tenure on the job but didn't share the same overachiever attitude as Jim. Nonetheless, he left the room with no more questions asked.

There were no problems that evening, only a more efficient approach by a young ambitious airman working the tower to save several new B-29 pilots time in their training. In fact, he was noticed by some of the pilots for his canny work, which was recognizably out of the norm of how things were usually done. Many of them had landed on the base numerous times before with much less communication and efficiency. They played off his lead from the tower, quickly realizing the new kid in town.

Jim enjoyed working the tower because it was a constant reminder of where he was going. The sight of planes landing and leaving the runway made him feel right at home. He especially liked to watch the sleek fighter jets depart out of sight, slowly fading into the rich Texas sky, like a mother welcoming her absent child back into her arms. That was an embrace he couldn't wait to feel, one only the most elite pilots do.

None too soon, January 29 came. He packed his belongings to make the half-hour drive across San Antonio to Lackland AFB where he would begin the first phase of Aviation Cadet Pilot Training—preflight. At that time, Randolph and Lackland were separate bases. It wasn't until 2010 that they merged along with US Army Fort Sam Houston to form what is now known as Joint Base San Antonio.

Lackland AFB originated during the Second World War, on June 15 1941, as part of Kelly Field before it became the San Antonio Aviation Cadet Center on 8 January 1943. The War Department constituted and activated the Seventy-Eighth Flying Training Wing (preflight), assigning it to the Army Air Forces Central Flying Training Command and providing aviation cadets the mechanics and physics of flying. Cadets were required to pass courses in mathematics and the hard sciences. Also known as ground school, students were taught aeronautics, deflection shooting, and thinking in three dimensions before ever entering an aircraft.

The Aviation Cadet Pilot Training Program was started in 1907 by the US Army Signal Corps to grow air assets of the army, long before the US Air Force became its own military branch on 18 September 1947, only five years prior to Jim enlisting. Candidates originally had to be between the ages of nineteen and twenty-five. They had to be athletic and honest. The program stopped training pilots in 1961 and navigators in 1965, before the US Air Force began relying on the USAF Academy, Reserve Officer Training Corps, and Officer Candidate School to provide pilots and aircrews, which were getting fewer in number all the time. Due to the onset of the new technological era since the introduction of the jet fighter, more focus was put on degreed recruits from the aforementioned elite institutions.

During the time Jim went through it, it was an interesting time because aircraft evolved from propellers to jet engines, changing the fighter business forever. The US Air Force was still new, yet it was advanced, and the Aviation Cadet Pilot Training Program birthed by the US Army was nearing the end of fifty-plus years of existence.

The Aviation Cadet Pilot Training Program produced so many leaders who forged the cornerstone for the United States Air Force, and it's important to understand that rich heritage. Pilots, navigators, and bombardiers who stood for American freedom throughout WWI, WWII, the Korean War, and much of the Vietnam War were products of the program that stood strong for half a century. According to *Air Force Officers Personnel Policy Development,* by 1970, twenty-five years after the end of World War II, over half of USAF general officers then on duty were cadet program graduates.

During the time Jim was starting preflight, eight years post-WWII and six months before the end of the Korean Conflict or the early Cold War period, the United States was in the process of demobilization. It's estimated that the cadet program trained 5,000 pilots annually from 1948 to the end of the program compared to 41,666 cadets who graduated each year during the years of WWII. The heavy surplus of pilots after the Second World War led to more stringent requirements from fewer cadets making the cut. At the very time Jim started preflight, it was estimated that only 1,800 enlisted men had qualified for the program. Out of those who finished, only the top percentile of the basic phase (the third training phase) qualified to fly fighter jets, which demanded stronger technical and physical abilities.

Jim's focus after January 29 was to graduate preflight (phase one) in order to achieve designation of aviation cadet and go on to primary flight school (phase two) for pilot training to fly a plane for the first time. After that was basic (phase three), where it was most important to remain at the top of the class before receiving wings and being commissioned. Last would be advanced training (phase four), where those with wings go to a specialized school fit for specific abilities and interest. Gunnery school was the goal or, more specifically, the gunnery school equipped with F-86 fighters—the plane that had gained great popularity in the Korean War against the MiG-15.

Phase one began when Jim pulled up to the barracks then walked through the door to find a line of bunks in perfect order throughout the single large room. He got there early and found his bunk right away. Only a few men were there, but one approached Jim with an enthusiastic handshake and introduction. "I'm Charlie Johnson from Lexington, Kentucky," he said. The introduction was reciprocated with, "Good to meet you, Charlie. I'm Jim."

More cadets filled the room over the next hour to take their assigned bunk. Loud with chatter, the room suddenly quieted when an older gentleman walked through the main door. Civilian instructors were contracted by the USAF for ground school to teach the basics, and standing before the cadets in regular clothes was one of those instructors.

"Good evening, cadets. I'm one of your instructors, and I want everyone to pay close attention," he said. "You'll be expected to rise early and get out the door quickly, but not before your area is neat and clean, bed made to standard for evaluation. We'll meet at 0600 for an early breakfast, where you'll find your assigned seat in the chow hall, and gain more instruction on how we eat square meals together."

He might have been a civilian, but he obviously had military experience, and it showed.

After a sound night's sleep, morning came not far behind the screech of a loud speaker that echoed the room with marching tunes. Beds were made, some better than others, and the new cadets filed out the exit to the chow hall next door.

Once everyone was seated, serving dishes were brought to the cadet at the head of the table. He took each one and helped himself before passing to the person left of him. The dishes went around clockwise, giving those sitting closest left of the head seat their food first. As plates were passed, the commander took the podium in front of the room to give further instruction on the day ahead and a quick rundown on eating instructions. Jim had seated himself next to the head of the table, but to his right—the very last spot to be served. He later found, even though he was last, that the food came out fresher and untouched, so even if he could complain, he wouldn't bother. Besides, they wouldn't be able to dig in anyway.

As it turned out, eating square meals was symbolic of the motion in which they ate. Cadets were to make the perfect shape of a square from plate to mouth, almost robotic in nature. It was a way to build consistency and further unity between them. It was a form of teaching discipline to achieve a goal at the expense of comfort.

After the first square meal, they marched to the lecture hall where they started studies. They were desperate to learn to fly, but they would never get any closer to an airplane than a picture of one during this phase.

After class ended the first day, they all learned firsthand what was expected of them when making their beds in the morning. The bed-making standards required the bounce of a quarter. If the quarter didn't bounce, the bed was ripped apart, earning its maker a gig equating to an hour-long walk as reprimand. Preflight was basic training all over again, except this time, as a potential officer and gentleman, hence more sophistication was required.

Get up, make your bed, put on your uniform, clean up your area before breakfast, and start studying, but do it in the right demeanor—one with formality. Practically every one of them walked off a gig after the first bed inspection. It's been said that the things you recall the most are those that hurt the worst; preflight instilled that philosophy.

Studying topics of flying with no actual flying time was a place to start. Jim knew it was a time to impress, so he watched his step all the way, overdelivering on everything asked of him. Cadets received rank based on their performance, so he always strived to be the best at everything, and there was no room for error. Some wouldn't make it through the first phase.

After three rigorous months of study, Jim reached the upper echelon of his class as a cadet lieutenant, allowing him to move on to primary training on 1 April 1953. Charlie was with him step-by-step, and the two became fast friends, and they still are to this day. Both excelled but had different long-term goals in mind.

The Korean War was notoriously known for air-to-air jet fighter conflict or dogfighting between the MiG-15 and F-86 at an incredibly high rate of speed. Jim was hell-bent on training in the F-86 then transitioning straight to war. He believed that if one didn't know exactly what they wanted, they would end up with something else, and he wanted jets.

Charlie was cut from the same mold, also being highly ambitious. However, great minds don't always desire the same things. Jim had his sights on shooting down MiG-15 enemies from the cockpit of an F-86 Sabre. Charlie, on the other hand, was more interested in air-to-ground tactics while flying something larger in size or, more specifically, flying the mega-size B-29 Superfortress that gained great fame toward the end of the Second World War and again in Korea. Charlie liked the bombers.

Neither would have the chance at training in their quintessential aircraft until completing basic though, and that was several phases beyond where they were.

After preflight, they were allowed a few days leave to visit family and eagerly give word on their achievements. Charlie, coming from a family who flew and actually owned an airplane back in Kentucky, had spent time recreational flying, and for him to share the news with them was something familiar.

Jim, on the other hand, had never been around airplanes until he'd stood next to as many as he could at Keesler AFB. To fly, as he was about to do in primary training at Spence Air Base in Moultrie, Georgia, was something he had only dreamed of just a year ago. Phase two would introduce the T-6 Texan and PA-18 aircraft that he and Charlie, along with the rest of the cadet class, would be required to each fly for 130 hours combined before a final military check ride to confirm readiness.

The trip home was quick and much-needed. After catching up with his family and new fiancée, he drove to Moultrie to report as a cadet with class 54 H under the Hawthorne School of Aeronautics established in May 1951. Jim's class was only the seventeenth class to go through the new Spence Field operation, Hawthorne School of Aeronautics, which quickly built a reputation for turning out some of the best officer pilots in the air force.

Living quarters were different than preflight, with assigned rooms shared between three guys rather than one large room for everyone. Charlie Johnson and Homer Hess from Uvalde, Texas, were Jim's new roommates.

Quickly establishing good rapport, they began to open up as people do once getting familiar through time together. Homer was a confident Texan who grew up privileged on a large ranch in Uvalde. He tried following the rules like Jim and Charlie, but sometimes, he found the gray area where he made his own. Not even a fighter pilot yet, he was about to drop a bomb. "I'm already married. Here's a picture of my wife," he said, then showed his roommates her photo. Cadets were not allowed to marry until they graduated, received their wings, and were commissioned. This was awkward news, but his secret remained safe with them. They knew he was one to press the limits, so they watched him closely as friends should, all the time trying to stay out of the way of any aftermath.

Homer was a trailblazer and fashion trendsetter with great swagger and an extensive wardrobe consisting of more than one pair of shoes, something that was out of the norm for other cadets of this generation. He dressed sharp and liked to see his roommates do the same, so he wasn't tightfisted with his clothes. Jim and Homer wore the same size shoe, allowing Jim to wear some of the best-quality shoes found in the United States and perhaps Italy. They were grain leather with stitched soles; they were nice, like walking on clouds. But more realistically, it was time for Jim and the others to sail over clouds by way of something less grounded than Homer or his shoes. The day came for their first aircraft experience—the PA-18 single-prop plane. However, they wouldn't go alone.

As beginners, cadets were trained to fly in dual situations, where their instructor sat tandem in the rear seat of the plane. Once meeting the initial requirement of flying dual with an instructor for one hundred hours, they were allowed to go solo—a big step forward. Flying alone for thirty hours was an obligation to be met without an instructor in the cockpit, something they built up to. They checked out in the P-18 first and then advanced to the T-6 Texan, which was a more powerful plane larger in size. Jim remembers that flying for the first time in the P-18 with an instructor was exhilarating but relatively uneventful; the same went for his solo in it. His first solo in the T-6 Texan, however, was different.

Reflecting back, he started by saying, "It was more airplane than the PA-18, and if you can fly the T-6 Texan, you can fly just about any single-prop. It's more of a challenge for a new guy." Like yesterday, he remembers sitting in the cockpit of the plane before takeoff, his instructor standing on the wing and making sure he was strapped in right while walking him through basic instructions. As Jim conferred with his instructor, Charlie Havill, a contracted civilian, they noticed another cadet bringing a T-6 in for landing. He hit the runway, lost control of the nose, and spun out, doing what is called a ground loop. In simpler terms, it looked like an out-of-control 360-degree circle at a high rate of speed. The young cadet ran off the runway into a cloud of dust before coming to a halt he wasn't in control of. Havill said, "Look at that! He just ground looped. He lost control of his rudders, so whatever you do, don't do that." Jim, with his eyes wide open, grinned with acknowledgment and then slid the canopy shut to prepare for takeoff. *This shouldn't be a hard act follow*, he thought to himself.

Taxiing over the asphalt runway while adjusting the rudders to ideal position, Jim built his speed and departed the runway in flight. His destination was a planned course near and around the base. It was always an empowering feeling to solo, and the more he did it, the more comfortable he got. The first time he soloed in the T-6, the sky was as clear and calm as Jim's head. It was one experience that he recalls most early on.

After the near hour solo, he brought the plane in for landing. On final approach, he kept full attention to keeping control of the rudders so as not to ground loop like the other young pilot, who obviously was feeling too comfortable. Touching down like a feather, he taxied the T-6 back in position to debrief with his instructor. Debriefing was standard routine throughout the progression of gaining flight time.

Jim, Charlie, and Homer accomplished topmost achievement in primary, reaching solo status in the PA-18 and T-6 Texan, fulfilling their requirements in six months, and readying them for their check ride. They completed the classroom curriculum covering the mechanical makeup of the aircraft and its purpose before a written examination.

The military check ride involved an experienced air force pilot testing them on difficult procedures including acrobatics such as aileron rolls, barrel rolls, lazy eights, reverse rollouts, and recovery tactics from engine failure. Instrument testing included an under-the-hood test, where they were required to fly while depending solely on instruments, unable to see out of the cockpit due to a literal hood covering their head. Some cadets struggled with this test, and they even washed out of the program after reaching the point.

Navigation testing during day and nighttime hours was a critical part of the check ride, along with takeoffs and landings. This type testing is an ongoing annual occurrence for air force pilots every time they are introduced to a new aircraft. Constant evaluation is necessary, even for the highest-level pilots. Two-seated planes accommodate check pilots with a backseat, and for one-seated planes, the check pilot flies the tester's wing to check proficiency. Many times, after becoming a pilot, check rides are performed with no notice—again showing the importance of a pilot being ready at any moment. There's no end to preparation for a fighter pilot.

In primary training, cadets were given notice of their check ride, and the second phase of the Aviation Cadet Pilot Training Program came to term. Jim, Charlie, and Homer all passed check rides with grace. Charlie was the first in class 54 H to solo, Jim was second, and Homer was thereafter. To this day, soloing first is a bragging right for Charlie, something Jim can live with because he always hoped the best for his friends while keeping a competitive nature. Another occurrence that took place during primary which he had a harder time living with was how the Korean War ended on 27 July 1953, before he got a chance to go. There was never another air war in terms of dogfighting like the Korean War.

JETS

It was October 1953 when they entered the third and final stage of the Aviation Cadet Program—basic flight training. Jim and Charlie remained roommates at Webb AFB in Big Spring, Texas, staying there until graduation in April of 1954. With two to a room, Homer was assigned a new roomie but stayed close to Jim and Charlie, all part of class 54-H. If they completed phase three, they would be commissioned as officers, receive their pilot wings, then attend advanced training to transition into their new specialty aircraft. In Jim's case, he was hopeful for advanced gunnery school in the F-86F fighter; a topflight finish would be required.

For basic, cadets kept the same itinerary as primary, with half a day for lecture and the second half for flying. They learned to fly in formation, fly by instruments (aerial navigation), fly at night, and fly for long distances. Basic required fifty-five hours in more sophisticated planes like the T-28 Trojan, spinning a single-prop accompanied by folding landing gear in the wings and nose.

Flying the T-28 through the first part was a slightly different experience. The plane required additional steps during takeoff and landed with a top speed of 280 miles per hour, larger and faster than the T-6. It sat level on the runway with a nose wheel, something different from the P-18 and T-6, which had tail wheels.

Once class 54-H checked out in the T-28, they took a big step up in the plane that followed. The T-33, being the first jet trainer, was a far more powerful plane than anything they had experienced. The T-33A Shooting Star, known as the T-Bird, was jet powered by an Allison J-33 engine and handled like a hot rod compared to the other training planes. Introduced to the air force in September 1948, an estimated 90 percent of the free world's military jet pilots trained in the T-33A during the 1950s and 1960s. The Lockheed war bird measured a sleek thirty-seven feet eight inches from nose to tail, spanning a nearly equal wingspan of thirty-seven feet six inches. At a top speed of roughly 525 miles per hour and with a ceiling of forty-five thousand feet, it was the most widely used advanced jet trainer in the world through August 1959. It was also the plane utilized in the movie that inspired Jim during his first date with Jeanie.

Flying it wasn't any different—you used the same principles taught to operate the other aircraft—but handling the quickness of a jet versus a propelled plane required more instinctive response. "Centerline thrust made the jet easier to fly in terms of directional control. There's no prop pulling the plane one way or the other. The jet thrust was displaced evenly, and there was a lot of it," said Jim. The power and speed of the T-33 could be unforgiving to error, leaving a young pilot little to no time to compensate for a hasty mistake. Absolute awareness was needed at all times when flying one. It took the lives of many young pilots in training.

Now on February 1954, a series of bad occurrences happened. Charlie and Jim were up early as usual. Their beds made to perfection. Charlie would solo the first half of the day, and Jim would fly that evening. Headed out the door first was Jim, en route to breakfast before going to the classroom. Later, he heard about all that happened from Charlie. Charlie had stayed behind to grab a few things he needed for flying when he heard a knock on the door. It was Homer, who seemed overly excited.

Homer had been especially happy they were near the end of basic flight training, for all the same reasons as everyone else. He'd told his buddies that he was especially glad he would no longer have to hide his secret marriage, which he was ready to get back to; he'd missed his wife dearly. He'd stepped inside to tell Charlie they were scheduled to solo at the same time that morning and that he had what he thought was the perfect idea.

"Charlie, lets fly in formation in the T-33s like we were taught a few weeks ago to my family's mountain cabin north of our ranch in Uvalde," said Homer. His wife was there, and he was anxious to see her face from the cockpit of the jet. Showing off was something he liked to do, and after all, he reminded Charlie, it wasn't bragging if you could back it up.

Charlie had quickly realized this was another example of the gray area Homer always managed to gravitate toward. Could they pull it off logistically? Maybe. But would it get them kicked out of the program if they were found out? The answer was yes. Could they die in the process? Yes. There was a good chance taking a jet they were hardly used to into a mountainous area could kill them both.

Charlie respectfully declined and then sincerely tried to talk Homer out of it. "I am certain you don't even have enough fuel to make that flight," he said. Homer insisted he was wrong then told Charlie, in his own choice words, that he was a pilot with no sense of adventure. Next, he stormed out and proceeded down the hallway, disgruntled. As Charlie watched him walk away, he'd thought, *I hope he doesn't go.* Little did he know, that would be the last time he would see Homer.

Jim caught Charlie on his way out of the chow hall. He told Charlie that he had just seen Homer, who'd asked him if he would fly back home to buzz his parents' cabin in the mountains the next time they were scheduled to fly together. Charlie said, "That's funny. He just came up to our room and asked me to do the same thing, and we're scheduled to fly together in less than forty-five minutes from now." Jim asked what was said exactly. "He called me a chicken shit then stormed off," said Charlie with a solemn look.

"When I told him no, he called me the same thing," said Jim. "If you see him before you board, make sure he's not serious, Charlie."

Charlie did see Homer climb into the cockpit of the trainer jet on the ramp minutes later, but it was too late. He made eye contact with Homer then shook his head, hoping to get through one last time, but like prey into the mouth of a predator, Homer climbed up into the fully fueled twelve-thousand-pound jet.

On the runway, Charlie watched his friend fly away, hoping he would see him again; even if he had to listen to him brag, he wanted to see him again.

During the hour-long training flight, Charlie couldn't help but worry about Homer's fate. He was on final approach for landing when he heard over his emergency radio that one of their T-33s had gone down near Uvalde. He kept his focus on the runway as he touched down with a heavy heart. He knew it was Homer; he just hoped that he was able to eject or somehow survive.

All the cadets flying that morning made their way back to the debriefing area where instructor, Major Gerard Rooney, called them into an uncommon emergency meeting. "Gentlemen, I have very bad news. One of your classmates was killed in a crash. The report says that a T-33 jet went down in a mountain valley near Uvalde, and it was the plane Homer Hess left in this morning. He was pronounced dead on impact," said Major Rooney.

He went on to say that if any of the cadets wanted to go buzzing or thought of taking one of the T-33s out for fun, to let him know, and he would take them himself. Rooney reminded everyone in the room that no one was qualified to go on their own.

Charlie left the silent room with anguish and regret. He and Jim had both tried to talk Homer out of it. Now he was dead.

Charlie broke the news to Jim. "You've got to be kidding me," Jim said. Both the young men were agonizing over whether they could have done anything else to prevent the tragedy, but ultimately, they knew how Homer was responsible. There would have been nothing in the world they could have said to change his mind. Homer did what he wanted to. He wasn't one you could tell what to do.

One thing was crystal clear. The airplane they were now flying was to be respected, something they wished Homer would have understood sooner. Charlie and Jim drove Homer's car home for the funeral with his belongings in the back. On their way there, Charlie took a sharp curve too fast, resulting in running the car off the road into the ditch without anyone getting hurt. It was if Homer was still with them, mixing it up even after he was gone. It took them a while to realize he wasn't.

The class of 54 H went on without Homer. His friendship, fellowship, and stubborn nature would be missed. Soon, many of the cadets would become air force officers without him, Jim and Charlie knew he would have made a good one with some fine-tuning. This was a constant reminder of what was at stake. Making the wrong move at any given time could cost the ultimate price. Flying fighter jets was not for the average lackadaisical soul. Living the life of a jet fighter pilot required respect for oneself and respect for the aircraft.

Nearing the end of their required time in the T-33, Jim was assigned a solo nighttime cross-country flight from Big Spring to El Paso, one of the more advanced exercises during basic. Leaving Webb AFB at dusk, he climbed the jet to thirty-five thousand feet, a good cruising altitude that made for an exhilarating feeling. Alone in the aircraft, he could hardly feel the earth moving past at five hundred miles per hour. He thought of the first time he had seen the plane he was now flying on the movie screen in Kansas; it was a dream come true.

At that very moment, a sense of accomplishment rushed his body, raising the hair on his arms. He could see El Paso glowing through the dark sky, bright city lights radiating in the distance. Jim, in a self-satisfied state, was momentarily lost in a trance. His eyes fixed on the glow, he soon realized how close he was getting to his destination. Glancing at his altitude gauge, he shockingly noticed he dropped to thirty thousand feet unaware. Before he could react, he was at twenty-five thousand feet. He snapped out of it and quickly adjusted his flying attitude to put the plane into a climb, bringing up the nose. Next, he accelerated power to regain altitude until he was in the correct position again. This was a lesson that he never forgot—paying close attention at all times and never letting your mind drift, not even for a second. After he straightened out his course, he analyzed where he had gone wrong, realizing he had focused his sights on the city below for too long and not paid attention to his gauges. "If you look at something long enough, you'll naturally fly toward it, similar to the way you inherently steer a car in the direction your eyes are fixed," said Jim.

Furthering his route while willing his heart rate to return to normal, he began correspondence with the flight control tower to clear his way back to Big Spring for landing and complete his night cross-country test.

With the slight lesson he learned that night, he couldn't help but think about the critical mistake Homer had made, but Jim understood how his friend had gotten in over his head and tragically crashed. Even though the emotion of losing a friend entered his mind, he never took his eyes off his altitude, staying fully conscious of his surroundings. When he reached Big Spring, he landed safely then debriefed with his instructor before turning in.

The following afternoon, Jim was right back in the T-33 to fly the last half of the day before dinner. Finishing the flight, he joined the rest of Class 54 H who all stood in attention outside the mess hall, awaiting their release for square meals.

Finally dismissed, they took off like a bolt of lightning. In front of the pack, closest to the door, was Jim. He had built a hearty appetite and was anxious to get to his seat. In full stride, just an arm's reach from the door, he felt a thrust of weight from behind. As the crowd of cadets who were trying to get through the same opening as him surged over his back, they crashed through the glass door like a battering ram, Jim at the nose. He hit the floor, buried by a pile of people. When they climbed back to their feet as orderly as possible, Jim, surfacing, last soon realized something dreadful. "Your hand is bleeding," another cadet said to him. Jim looked down at his lacerated wrist, discovering an awful wound. Then he pulled a triangular shard of glass deep from his punctured flesh, muscle, and tendons.

Initially, there was little blood visible, but when he cusped his hand over the opening with a good amount of pressure, he soon witnessed a crimson stream spewing between his fingers over his head. Jim couldn't move his blood-covered fingers, and he felt a tingling sensation run from the injured wrist up his arm. His next thought was, *How am I going to fly jets with one hand? They could wash me out, and I'll be done!* Several fellow cadets rushed Jim to the hospital.

It was confirmed his tendons were severed—the reason he had no movement in his fingers—so doctors reattached them during a three-hour emergency operation. The procedure was twofold—first, reattaching his parts piece by piece, which was fortunately possible, and second, connecting a tension screw to the fused tendons. This was for rehabilitation purposes, so the doctors could manually loosen and tighten his hand each week to help gain proper recovery. What seemed to be the best period of his life was now spiraling downward. He knew he had made a good impression on the hierarchy of the program and remained at the top of his class, yet the future remained uncertain. He was given the benefit of the doubt, but his destiny would hinge on complete recovery.

With back-to-back doctor appointments over the coming weeks, he kept up with the books while watching others fly. Then the day came to go in for the final procedure. He would have the tension screw released before a physical check. It was nerve-racking to say the least, and he hoped his entire hand didn't fall apart.

After the screw was taken out, he was asked to open and close his hand, which was totally numb. To his surprise, his hand curled into a half fist and opened right up with some effort, and he closed it the same way; it worked. Smiling, he opened and closed it with repetition until the doctor said, "Okay, you can stop now."

Jim was cleared to fly again, but not in time to graduate with Charlie and the rest of 54 H. He was put back a class to 54 J to make up for the time missed while healing. Jim and Charlie continued to room together up until the day Charlie graduated basic and went on to advanced training in Lake Charles, Louisiana, for bomber school in the B-29. The three roommates had started out together, determined to rule the sky in one way or another. But as fate would have it, the trio all went separate ways, with Homer Hess departing before ever receiving wings.

Jim continued to fly after being told he would always have a problem with nerve damage. "To this day, at age eighty-one, my wrist and hand have never bothered me except for some permanent numbness in the very lower part of my thumb. That's the extent of it," he said.

His transition to class 54 J was smooth, and he remained in the top of the new class as he had been with 54 H before the accident.

With his classroom time complete, he aced the written exam, only needing to finish flying time in order to do his check ride in the T-33. This also happened with no problems; the injury didn't interfere. When everyone completed testing and checkout flights, 54 J gathered for a final meeting before being commissioned and pinning on their wings.

The class, with sixty-seven cadets ready to graduate, met in the lecture hall, where a list of airplanes was posted on a board. It revealed plenty of jets to go around, including F-94s, F-89s, and F-84s, but there were only eight of the F-86F Sabres. Cadets were allowed to choose in the order of their ranking based on their performance in the class. Jim was in the top of the class, tenth overall, narrowing his chances for the F-86F if those before him picked it first.

When it was time for the first cadet to take his pick, he chose an F-84, putting Jim one step closer. It was looking good. The second pick followed suit, which guaranteed Jim an F-86 that he took without hesitation when it came to him. Some things were just meant to be.

Advanced Training or F-86 Gunnery School would take place at Nellis AFB in Las Vegas, Nevada, which Jim's soon-to-be-wife, Jeanine, had mentioned as a desirable place to live. It was something they would soon find out for themselves. He was commissioned as second lieutenant and had his wings pinned on his chest as a United States Air Force officer on 26 May 1954. He was now ready for the final step.

Jim and Jeanie married in Lyons, Kansas, on 30 May 1954, only four days after he finished basic. It was perfectly okay now that he was through the program. The new couple took a quick honeymoon in Dodge City then went back home to Lyons to spend some extra time with family before moving to Las Vegas to start a life together. Jim would begin advanced flight training with the 3394th Pilot Training Squadron at Nellis AFB on the first week of June 1954.

THE F-86

The newlyweds drove into the dry heat of Las Vegas on a Friday afternoon. A newly rented home awaited them on the north side of town, where they would spend the next ninety days. After the first night there, Jim was up early to tell Jeanie he was going to drive out to Nellis AFB to make sure he knew where he was going on Monday for advanced training; he was not taking any chances of being late for his first day.

Nellis Air Force Base was named on 30 April 1950, and by July 1, the air force had directed Air Tactical Command to accelerate Korean War training for a new ninety-five-wing air force. The first school opened at Nellis, and ATC redesignated the 3595th Pilot Training Wing (advanced single-engine) as the 3595th Training Wing for the F-86F at the time of Jim's arrival.

After a ten-minute drive to the base, he approached the gate, showed credentials, then got directions to the ops building. Pulling up, he saw several F-86F fighters standing strong, nose to tail on the ramp; it was a beautiful sight and a strong indicator he was in the right place. He parked his car then walked around the building to check the doors to see if he could get inside, but they all appeared to be locked. Then the last door he inspected slowly creaked open; he stepped inside and said, "Is anyone here?" From around the corner came a man in uniform. "Can I help you?"

After a brief conversation, Jim and the officer found out they would soon work together; the officer was a flight instructor for advanced training. Little did Jim know, it was John R. Boyd, who would later invent the OODA Loop (observe, orient, decide, and act), which is still used by the military and corporate world today. By chance, the two were there together that Saturday morning, preparing for the upcoming week. Boyd, being the initiator that he was, asked if Jim wanted to go ahead with the issue of his flight gear along with everything he would need a few days early. All F-86 Sabre pilots were required to wear G-suits, a flight suit designed to prevent a blackout or loss of consciousness caused by blood pooling in the lower part of the body when under extreme acceleration. Deprivation of blood to the brain can cause black-outs (G-LOC), leading many jet pilots to aircraft accidents, particularly with the coming of supersonic aircraft. It was later discovered that MiG-15 pilots did not wear G-suits, giving US pilots a major advantage in the Korean War.

Jim gladly accepted and then Boyd blew him away with something else. "Since you're here early, would you like to go ahead and take your first ride in the F-86 today?"

After the fitting and equipment issuance, the two stepped out on the ramp behind the ops (squadron) building for a quick rundown. Jim approached the beautiful fighter with great admiration. Over thirty-seven feet long, with swept wings measuring thirty-seven feet from tip to tip, the single General Electric J-47-GE-27 turbojet powered the Sabre to speeds of 687 miles per hour at sea level when weighing the perfect combat weight of 14,212 pounds. This plane was the United States' answer to the Russian MiG-15. It was able to go supersonic speeds in a dive, which was an advantage over the Russian jet, which, as they later found out, couldn't.

The silver Sabre glistened in the Nevada sun. Its armor-plated tail was distinctly marked by a black-on-yellow checkerboard pattern. Each side of the fuselage proudly displayed the red, white, and blue US aircraft insignia—a white star circled in blue and spawned white horizontal bars on both sides, accented by a single red stripe down the center of each; it was symbolic of American wings.

Jim had never been so close to the world-renowned jet. The realization of him flying it was truly a monumental moment. His checkout in the T-33 was the preparation he needed. It was also a privilege to be given an opportunity at such a feat as the F-86. He had successfully learned to fly and maneuver at the highest rates of speed available to man within the stratosphere. However, everything he had piloted to this point had been unarmed.

The F-86F was equipped with six Browning AN/M3 .50-caliber machine guns, modified with an electrically boosted feed mechanism to increase the rate of fire to near 1,200 rounds per minute. The cannons were stocked with cameras in order to photograph targets, a useful tool in meeting requirements for confirmed kills. Every official kill had to be confirmed by a second pilot or photographic proof since fighter pilots sometimes faced combat alone.

Equipped with a radar range gun sight capable of locking on to targets electronically, an enemy MiG had little chance of escaping once an F-86 was zeroed in. The swept wings were designed with two Matra rocket pods to launch eighteen 68 mm rockets per pod. There was ample room for 5,300 pounds of payload on four external hard points, where bombs were usually mounted on the outer two pylons as the inner pairs were plumbed for two 200–US gallon drop tanks that gave the Sabre a more useful range. Dropping fuel tanks then going to internal fuel supply provided passage back to United States or allied soil without extra weight. The increased tankage added an extra twenty minutes to the F-86F in the combat zone. Similar to racing, minimizing weight while maximizing distance and speed was important in the fighter business, something Boyd would eventually be known for in the history of fighter design.

A wide variety of bombs could be carried (max standard load-out being two 1,000 lb. bombs plus two drop tanks), or napalm canisters. The jet was a $211,111 weapon platform built specifically for combat. Under the control of the most trained and qualified pilots, it was a lethal weapon when airborne. American flying aces were an elite group on the rise due to the Korean War; the best were known as MiG killers. They were as notorious as professional baseball players, requiring more skill and a fearless yet calculated demeanor. For a fighter pilot, an error was more than giving up a ground ball with the bases loaded. An error in the matchup of air-to-air-combat meant the loss of life. They were admired by all, disrespected by few, loved by most, and feared by the enemy.

When walking on the ramp around the F-86F with Boyd by his side, Jim realized he was now in the big show, soon to get a chance to play in the World Series of air-to-air combat.

Jim and Boyd performed the preflight walk around of the F-86 he was going to fly, a standard procedure prior to starting up any fighter.

Jim climbed into the cockpit to strap it on. Any good fighter pilot not only fastened in by harness, he strapped on the airplane as if he was one with it. It was something taught to all, yet it was only fully embraced by a MiG killer and those who wanted to be. Boyd stood on a ladder outside of the jet to show him how to start the F-86 and then set all the switches necessary to taxi to the runway for takeoff.

Once Jim settled in, Boyd approached and boarded his 86 next to Jim's. He started the jet and radioed, "We'll taxi out to runway 36. Follow me and remember the nose wheel steering button at the bottom of the grip on your control stick." This was the first plane Jim had flown with nose wheel steering. The others were steered by tapping the brakes.

Boyd then called the tower for taxi and takeoff instructions and said, "Follow me." They proceeded out as Jim had done many times before, but this time, he was in the world's most sophisticated fighter jet. He couldn't stop grinning; he loved every minute of it.

As they reached the end of the runway, they were cleared on for takeoff. Just as Jim was briefed prior, he lined up on Boyd's right wing for a formation takeoff, which he was familiar from his earlier T-33 training. Again, the difference was, this time, he was sitting in a world-class sports car, not a four-door sedan. This became even more and more apparent when he began to roll for takeoff.

With 5,910 lbs. force-of-thrust power, the F-86 accelerated much faster, and the controls were as sensitive as an iPad's screen. He quickly found out this was an advantage in keeping positioned. As they left the ground together, Jim stayed in close formation. Climbing to thirty thousand feet in 5.2 minutes was a breeze. Staying in close formation, they cruised at 599 miles per hour. Their range was 463 miles on internal fuel, and Jim held the wing position so tight that you would have thought they were attached. He stayed close through various maneuvers, in absolute amazement by the speed and agility of the fighter plane.

Performing all sorts of formations—close, route, spread, and offensive and defensive positions—Jim mirrored every acrobatic measure in absolute rhythm, even doing so without using power when prompted by Boyd. One hour passed without him knowing it. Then Jim heard, "Close back in route formation two-by-four ship widths, and I'll show you the local area including the ranges where you'll learn how to shoot while here at Nellis." After buzzing the ranges at a lower altitude, Boyd instructed Jim to move back into close formation, wingtip clearance only. He led them back into the traffic pattern for a few touch and goes before calling it a wrap.

Entering the traffic pattern at Nellis AFB is a standard procedure for all bases, using ground checkpoints and altitudes over each point to position the flight.

Jim, with his 86 in close right echelon formation, took five seconds from the 180-degree break Boyd made on the downwind leg before following to base leg and then to final before touching down on the runway with him.

This type of landing can be done with one aircraft or more, but usually, the number is one to four. Like clockwork, they touched down at the same point, five to seven seconds apart, in the center of the runway.

Once landing, they rolled to the end of the runway, taxied back to the ramp, and parked the aircraft in the same spots they found them. Now back where they belonged, if the planes had no write-up (problems) after inspection, they were usually left in the same space for refueling and then made ready for the next day's use. These particular 86s stayed put, in perfect condition for refueling.

Everything Jim experienced from the flight, including maneuvers and entering the pattern for landing and touching down, was as he had been taught, and flying the F-86F went very well. It was a great first flight in a world-class fighter plane. He couldn't wait until it was time to hit the ranges and open fire on targets. That was the end goal of gunnery training—learning how to shoot and drop live ordinance while maneuvering. Those who achieved that with perfection stayed in the F-86, and those who were not as accomplished were assigned to other types of aircraft that moved at slower rates of speed.

"To tell you how proud I was, I'm still in awe of it all," said Jim over sixty years later. This is a modest statement from someone who would later fly 377 combat missions in the Vietnam War, but he really liked the airplane, especially at that time.

After walking off the ramp, Boyd debriefed with Jim, telling him how well he did for a first flight in the F-86. He was proud that Jim would be part of the program with them. "Between me and you, no one really knows what it's like to fly a fighter like the F-86 unless they've done it. People have asked me through the years, and I try to describe it, but it's really not possible to do so in words. The only way to really know is to earn the wings required to do it, which is something that fewer and fewer are doing in today's air force. It's not the same today as it was then," Jim says.

"All I could think of was, 'I did it,' remembering back to that night at the movie theater, watching the picture *Air Cadet* in late 1951 and all that followed through 1952 and '53 to this moment in June 1954.

"I never doubted that I could as long as I stayed focused and determined and believed in myself. After all, I'm just playing the part of me in the master plan of my life. Who could do it better?"

Learning to fly was the easiest thing Jim had ever done. Now the hard part was about to begin. Learning to use the fighter plane for what it was built for and developing the skills necessary to make that second nature was to come over the next three months. He was ready.

As Jim and Boyd walked back to the facilities where they would sit and talk a while longer, Jim noticed the big black chalkboard that hung in the large lecture room as they passed by. He inquisitively asked, "What's the board for?"

"It's a running list of US pilots from Korea who had confirmed kills,' said Boyd. At the top of the list were Joseph McConnell, James Jabara, and Frederick Blesse—the top three US pilots with the most kills. When Jim thought the day couldn't get any better, he got the most encouraging news a young fighter pilot could imagine.

"Yes," said the instructor, "I heard confirmation today that Frederick Blesse, back home from Korea, has been assigned to our base here at Nellis to help with instruction on training you guys in the F-86F."

He went on to say, "He and Robbie Risner, another ace a little further down the list with eight confirmed kills, will be part of the special instruction here. Blesse has authored a fighter tactics book called *No Guts, No Glory* that we'll use as part of your training. It's going to explain in explicit detail the basis of fighter combat operations, and we'll go through it with the experts who just returned from combat."

Jim arrived back home where Jeanie waited. She'd been wondering what in the world could have happened to him. He was only going to drive to the base to make sure he knew how to get there, and what should have taken less than an hour had turned into over three hours—this was way before the convenience of cell phones. Sometimes, a fighter pilot's wife had to wait through the unknown, but that wasn't going to be easy, particularly later on when she was waiting thousands of miles away while her husband was fighting for the country. You could say this was training for her as well. She loved Jim like crazy, so waiting to hear was a tall order she would have to learn to deal with.

He walked through the door, and she said, "Oh, thank goodness you're home! Did you get lost?"

Jim smiled and said, "No, but I did get a tour at thirty thousand feet in an F-86 with this great pilot I met named John Boyd who's just back from Korea. You wouldn't believe the sight of this place at six hundred miles per hour."

She could tell he was exuberant, and the last thing she wanted to do was take that from him. She smiled, sat down, and asked for him to keep on. "I want to hear more about this." She put her feelings aside and listened. Behind every successful man was a strong woman, and Jim had that.

Lying in bed that night, they talked for hours about what the future might look like.

PATRIOTS

Monday morning, Jim arrived with the other pilots to report for gunnery school. Greeting them was the commanding officer of the 3595th Combat Crew Training Group—Col. George L. Jones. The group was made up of the 94th, 95th, and 96th Training Group Fighter Squadrons, with a host of important people including the budding instructor Boyd, who'd taken Jim out in the F-86 early; Frederick Blesse; and Robbie Risner, who was visiting temporarily.

Robbie Risner arrived in Korea on May 10, 1952, assigned to the 15th Reconnaissance Squadron at Kimpo Air Base. In June, when the 336th Fighter-Interceptor Squadron, also at Kimpo, sought experienced pilots, he arranged a transfer to the 4th Fighter Wing.

His first two months of combat, he saw little contact with MiGs, and although a flight leader, he took a three-day leave to Japan in early August. When returning to Korea, he found enemy planes were operational in numbers. Arriving at Kimpo in the middle of the night, he joined his flight on alert status. The flight of four F-86 Sabres launched and encountered fourteen MiG-15s. In a brief dogfight, Risner shot down one to score his first aerial victory on August 5, 1952.

On September 15, Risner's flight escorted F-84 Thunderjet fighter-bombers attacking a chemical plant on the Yalu River near the East China Sea. During their defense of the bombers, Risner's flight overflew the MiG base at Antung Airfield, China, which led him into a heroic situation. Encountering a single MiG, he followed it at nearly supersonic speeds down a dry riverbed and across low hills to an airfield thirty-five miles inside China.

The MiG pilot was better than most, putting up a great challenge for Risner. However, he was relentlessly in pursuit of another kill. Whirling up dust from the riverbed, the enemy jet loomed in his gun sights. Scoring numerous hits on the MiG, which was shooting off its canopy, Risner chased the flaming MiG between hangars of the Communist airbase, where he shot it down into parked fighters on the enemy's base. He nosed the F-86 up over the blazing flames of the frenzied base. Through sporadic gunfire he climbed.

Like a bat out of hell on the return flight, Risner's wingman, 1st Lt. Joseph Logan, was struck in his fuel tanks by antiaircraft fire over Antung. In an effort to help him reach Kimpo, Risner attempted to push Logan's aircraft by having him shut down his engine to insert the nose of his own jet into the tailpipe of Logan's—an unprecedented and untried maneuver. The goal was to push Logan's aircraft to the island of Cho-do, off the North Korean coast, where the air force maintained a helicopter rescue detachment. His canopy was covered by spewing jet fuel, and hydraulic fluid making it impossible to see. Turbulence kept separating the two jets, but Risner was intent on guiding the wounded 86 out over the sea. He kept reconnecting his nose to the extinguished burner. Suddenly, loss of fluids threatened to stall Risner's engine as well. They were forced to separate for good.

"I'll see you at the base tonight," said Logan before bailing out near Cho-do. Although Logan came down close to shore and was a strong swimmer, he got caught up in his parachute and drowned. Risner's engine flamed out, and he glided to landing at Kimpo to find out Logan didn't make it.

On September 21, he shot down his fifth MiG, becoming the twentieth jet ace. In October 1952, Risner was promoted to major and named operations officer of the 336th FIS. He flew 108 missions in Korea and was credited with the destruction of eight MiG-15s, his final victory occurring on January 21, 1953.

Frederick Corbin "Boots" Blesse graduated from the United States Military Academy in 1945. He flew two combat tours during the Korean War, completing 67 missions in F-51s, 35 missions in F-80s, and 121 missions in F-86s. During the second tour in F-86s, he was officially credited with shooting down nine MiG-15s and one La-9. The Lavochkin La-9 was a Soviet fighter aircraft produced shortly after World War II, a piston-engine aircraft produced at the start of the jet age.

At the time of his return to the United States on October 1952, he was America's leading jet ace.

General Blesse remained with fighter aircraft for practically his entire military career. During the 1955 Air Force Worldwide Gunnery Championship, he won all six trophies offered for individual performance, a feat never equaled. The Worldwide Gunnery Meet (William Tell) is a biennial aerial gunnery competition with fighter aircraft held by the United States Air Force in every even-numbered year. It was named after William Tell, the Swiss archer who was compelled by an immoral prince to shoot at an apple from his son's head. As the story goes, Willy shot, split the apple, and secured his freedom. Tell was a man of precision under the most stressful conditions.

In the competition, teams representing the various major commands of the USAF competed in live-fire exercises, using towed banner targets for gun engagements and obsolete fighters converted into unmanned target drones (currently QF-4 Phantoms) for air-to-air missile engagements. In layman's terms, it's the Olympics for fighter pilots, something Jim would participate in later. It was held at Nellis AFB.

During his tours of duty in Korea, General Blesse wrote his fighter tactics book, *No Guts, No Glory.* This book has been used as a basis of fighter combat operations for the Royal Air Force, the US Marine Corps, Chinese Nationalist, Korean Air Force, and US Air Force since 1955. As recently as 1973, three thousand copies were reproduced and sent to tactical units in the field.

The budding training instructor Jim flew with, two days prior, was John Richard Boyd. He would turn out to be one of the most important air-to-air combat strategists with no combat kills in history. He had only flown a few missions in the last months of the Korean War, and all of them as a wingman. Wingmen fly behind lead and don't even turn their guns on without permission.

Despite no kills, the art of air-to-air combat was something he understood better than most. He was near the end of completing jet instructor upgrade training at the time he and Jim met, and he would soon serve as an instructor pilot with the 3597th Combat Crew Training Squadron. The morning he and Jim flew together, he wasn't officially an instructor, but he jumped at the chance to take a new jet pilot up to test his skills as a teacher.

Boyd had the ability to defeat any other pilot in a dogfight. In order to humble his students, he would allow them to get behind him in an ideal firing position, and within 40 seconds, he would maneuver himself so that the positions were reversed and he had the optimum position, winning the fight. He became known as Forty-Second Boyd and was never defeated.

Because of his position within the air force, Boyd was learning much about dogfighting, and that was why he was able to defeat every pilot he faced. However, without a degree in engineering, he would be unable to prove his theories, so he later earned the degree from Georgia Institute of Technology. He went on to write the *Aerial Attack Study*, which was his legacy to the dogfighters of the air force, as it provided a concise and scientific explanation of how to win a dogfight. Rather than a list of useful maneuvers as was used before, this study, which became the official dogfighting manual for the air force, showed pilots how to think several moves ahead of their opponents and also showed every move and countermove that a pilot could make.

In the early 1960's, with Thomas Christie, who was a civilian mathematician, Boyd created the energy-maneuverability theory or E-M theory of aerial combat. Known to ask for forgiveness rather than permission by reputation, Boyd was said to have stolen the computer time to do the millions of calculations necessary to prove the theory that became the world standard for the design of fighter aircraft.

He formed a small advocacy group within Headquarters USAF that dubbed itself the Fighter Mafia. Two of its members also made history. Everest Riccioni was an air force fighter pilot assigned to a staff position in research and development while Pierre Sprey was a civilian statistician working in systems analysis. Together, they were the masterminds who conceived the LFX Lightweight Fighter program, which ultimately produced both the F-16 and McDonnell Douglas F/A-18 Hornet. The Fighter Mafia's ultimate goal was to design supreme fighter aircraft. The mathematical model they developed enabled quantitative (number-driven) one-to-one comparison of the performance of aircraft in terms of air combat maneuvering independent of real-world flight-testing; it was purely a statistical approach. The model was used to identify deficiencies with both designs in service and proposed designs of the time. Boyd, who had never flown a fighter with any type of avionics or radar, came down solidly on the side of sacrificing the weight of avionics for performance.

After he retired from the air force in 1975, he would continue to work at the Pentagon as a consultant in the Tactical Air office of the office of the assistant secretary of defense for Program Analysis and Evaluation.

He is credited for largely developing the strategy for the invasion of Iraq in the Gulf War of 1991. In 1981, Boyd had presented his briefing, Patterns of Conflict, to Dick Cheney, then a member of the United States House of Representatives. By 1990, Boyd had moved to Florida because of declining health, but Cheney (then the Secretary of Defense in the George H. W. Bush administration) called him back to work on the plans for Operation Desert Storm. Boyd had substantial influence on the ultimate design of the plan.

In a letter to the editor of *Inside the Pentagon*, former Commandant of the Marine Corps General Charles C. Krulak said, "The Iraqi army collapsed morally and intellectually under the onslaught of American and Coalition forces. John Boyd was an architect of that victory as surely as if he'd commanded a fighter wing or a maneuver division in the desert."

When Jim arrived for gunnery school, the talent present was of epoch-making.

As he walked in to take his seat, the other fifteen pilots were asked to fit for their gear, leaving some time on his hands since Boyd had taken care of that for him earlier. While waiting, he approached Blesse to introduce himself with his copy of *No Guts, No Glory* in hand that he picked up from his seat.

Despite his great success, Blesse was a humble man, and he asked Jim to hand him the copy of the book. At the top, he penned in something as he gave Jim verbal advice. "Jim, I'm going to give you a tip." He wrote this out in perfect penmanship: "Learn the tactics in this book and you might survive!" In the bottom right-hand corner, he noted, "For Lt. Jim Ryan, Nellis AFB." Although a celebrity—not to mention an American hero—he didn't autograph it. He was way too modest for that, and Jim wouldn't think of asking.

Worth mentioning also was the fact that commanding officer Jones was a United States Air Force flying ace during the Korean War, shooting down six enemy aircraft, with an additional shared victory credit, for a total of 6.5 victories in the war. He wrote the foreword for *No Guts, No Glory* and escaped death on many occasions while dogfighting with enemy MiG in Korea.

Although Blesse's official kill record was eight enemy aircraft, Jones gave him ten in the foreword of the book; there was always variance in the official number of kills for an ace. With Blesse experienced as a flight leader in combat and a squadron commander with ten confirmed kills, he was highly qualified to discuss air-to-air warfare with the young pilots as far as Jones was concerned. I'm pretty sure no one in the world would have questioned that.

On Jim's official first day of gunnery school, he realized right away that he had been taken under the wings of patriots, something that would reoccur throughout his career. He never looked back until the writing of this book.

From this morning forward, every pilot attending air defense command weapons training (gunnery school) would be required to obtain fifty-four hours on the ranges performing various training missions. They would practice offensive and defensive maneuvers consisting of high-altitude dogfights, high and low altitude bombing exercises, and even lower-altitude strafing runs with the .50-caliber machine guns zeroed in on either motionless or moving ground targets.

There were six wide-open ranges in the deserts of Nevada located ninety miles north of Nellis AFB in Indian Springs, which started as an Auxiliary Airfield that was rapidly constructed in Nevada the month after the Pearl Harbor attack. Indian Springs was immediately entered into service as a training camp for Army Air Force B-25 air-to-air gunnery training and as a divert field for Las Vegas Army Airfield. In 1947, Las Vegas AAF inactivated, and so did Indian Springs.

One year later, it was reactivated as Indian Springs Air Force Base, with a new role as a new weapons systems and aircraft research and testing site for nuclear arms, high-altitude balloon search and retrieval, and new gunnery and rocketry systems, as well as experimental aircraft. During the 1950s and 1960s, Indian Springs housed some of the most advanced aircraft and air weapons systems in the world.

Everyday flights of four took off to the ranges after an initial briefing to explain in detail the mission and expectations, each pilot being watched closely for a critical debriefing at return.

After the initial briefing, pilots left the operations building together for the ramp where they boarded their planes with close attention on lead. Once the instructor closed his canopy, two, three, and four followed simultaneously. Lead element would radio to start their engines, and each position answered back in sequence of order. At landing, no one opened their canopy until lead did. Flight formation started the minute you left the ops building, with everything in perfect timing behind lead. Number two pilot flew lead's wing—number three pilot became lead in a flight of two if the grouping of four split up into two separate flights—four remaining on his wing.

When taking off, lead and two roll together for takeoff while three and four roll together five to seven seconds behind. Two is always on the left of lead, and three and four are on the right. This is a right-hand fingertip formation, thumb back and four fingers forward—the index finger being number two man, the middle finger being lead, the next is three, and pinky is the four man.

Formations are so tight, timely, and uninterrupted that they look like a systematic arrangement. Tempo and consistency is a way of life for a fighter pilot. There is no other way to do it. Regardless if it's a flight of four or seventy-two, everything is timed in accordance.

During Jim's training, many times, his instructor, D.H. Lockwood would pair with a single ace like Risner or Blesse and two students to make four. They usually took a different route to the range each time before splitting up in two groups of two to have a high-altitude mock dogfight.

On return, they flew the same route back to enter the traffic pattern.

They did this day in and out while spending ample time in the classroom learning the material in *No Guts, No Glory* then discussing and debating air-to-air combat tactics in detail with the MiG Killers in the room to provide answers. It was invaluable experience for a young pilot, and getting to fly training missions with them was even better.

Nearing the end of advanced training, Jim recalls one of the more difficult lessons learned in the F-86F.

He had spent a day in Indian Springs perfecting a tactic called skip bombing—flying near the ground at low altitude carrying twenty-five-pound bombs dropped at the perfect speed, altitude, dive angle, and bombsight settings and skipping the ordnance forward to explode, similar to the way a rock is skipped off the water. It was something initially developed after Pearl Harbor to hit the sides of Imperial Japanese Navy Warships by skipping bombs into them off of the sea.

After the bombing exercise, the flight of four decided to take it back up to thirty thousand feet to spar a little on the fuel they had left before going back to base. Pushing the right rudder and then the left, lead waggled his tail as a signal for the flight to breakup into flights of two. Jim and his wingman paired up, Jim in lead. They faced off against Lockwood and Risner for a dogfight.

Meeting nose to nose, with a hundred-foot separation at over five hundred miles per hour, the two teams raced in a vertical climb to gain the outside position, an advantage when dogfighting. Lockwood and Risner climbed hard. Jim and his wingman, with a slight edge, gained the best angle of attack.

Lockwood and Risner, realizing they were at a disadvantage, rolled out left. Jim and his wingman held tight, not giving up any distance and gaining more inside. Jim locked in his sights in such a way he could have shot to kill, had he been in a real combat situation.

Lockwood radioed, "Nice job, Ryan. I'm afraid you got me."

Risner echoed, "That's affirmative. Nice work, guys."

Rocking his wings, Lockwood signaled Jim and his wingman to group back in formation of four so they could head back to base on the fuel they had left.

They did so, and the four F-86Fs roared toward Nellis over the halfway point in an area called the green spot, which was used as a reference point.

Jim started gradually falling back, and everything started to unravel as he noticed lead, two, and four leaving him behind at a fast rate. Next, he realized his power was gone. He knew he had flamed out. With his engine dead, he broke the silence of the radio. "Lead, I've flamed out. I've tried restarting with no success."

Lockwood told him to gain as much altitude as he could and head to base. Breaking the traffic pattern they were in, Jim had no choice but to head dead east toward the runway. With no power, he nosed it over and started his glide at 180 knots toward Sunrise Mountain, which skirted the ten-thousand-foot runway, making a good reference point. Fortunately, he was cruising five hundred miles per hour prior to the glide at high altitude, so he could do this. The worst-case scenario was that he would be forced to eject, but bailing out of a fast-moving aircraft near a runway could cause extended devastation, not anything he wanted to resort to.

He called base, telling them he was going to land while flamed out, and then turned downwind, parallel with the mountain range. Careful not to give up too much speed too soon, he pulled hard into base leg and hit his airbrakes to decelerate. He couldn't give up speed too quickly because he wouldn't be able to get it back in the dead Sabre. Gliding into final approach while keeping his speed constant, Jim aligned with the end of the runway, knowing that any asphalt behind him was absolutely worthless. He descended nose down, slowly rounding it out and easing the nose back up into a landing attitude. His tires squawked against the asphalt; he stuck it down safely.

Jim had successfully accomplished a flameout landing in the 86, something that was only discussed in the classroom because it was too dangerous to try in real time. In his case, he didn't have a choice but to do one.

"The landing was near perfect, touching down slightly long. The instructor flew by just as I touched down, telling me to get it off the runway onto a taxiway as soon as speed would allow and to call the tower for a tug to a parking place to be checked by a maintenance crew. By the time I got it parked, my instructor had landed, parked, and was there to pick me up. What a good day and an even better outcome," said Jim. "It was a real backslapper."

FINISHING

The desolate desert ranges in Indian Springs Valley rumbled as flights of F-86s led by American flying aces performed live fire exercises atop targets with live ordnance. This was as close as a pilot could get to a live combat experience, but there was one component missing—the targets didn't fire back. However, the young Sabre pilots, trained to treat each mission as if they could in fact catch fire, rolled out after sinking their bombs into the bowls of the valley, clearing just seconds after each erupting blast.

Jim was learning to use the arsenal of weapons. Understanding the fighter business consisted of much more than just flying. Learning was accomplished through lecture, reading, reinforcing exercises, and testing.

That's how we learn, but there's something dynamic about an expert showing you firsthand the tricks of the trade, like the way a little league baseball player observes the swing of a major leaguer from behind home plate. Seeing is believing, and repeating the actions of others at the top of their game elevates the performance of the observer.

One morning, over the ranges, Jim was exposed to something that agreed with him indefinitely. It was late June 1954, and the worldwide Gunsmoke competition had started.

Held biennially, Gunsmoke was the USAF's worldwide gunnery meet run by the United States Tactical Fighter Weapons Center at Nellis, AFB. It tested the conventional air-to-surface capability of the combat air forces, recognizing the best aircrews, maintenance teams, and munitions load teams the world has to offer.

It began in 1949, purely from air-to-ground exercises, with emphasis placed heavily on accuracy in dive bombing, rocket delivery, and strafing with the gun in multiple demanding strike profiles.

The event brought together the best Tactical Air Forces' air-to-ground units from the United States and abroad for an intensive two-week extravaganza of flying, bombing, strafing, weapons loading, and aircraft maintenance events. To this day, these events are somewhat unique in that they measure precision not just in terms of bombing and strafing but also in terms of the many support personnel involved with servicing the aircraft used in competition. It's an opportunity for an entire team to display their skill.

Claire Patterson Chennault, the son of the great Claire Lee Chennault, was participating in the event out of Nellis AFB. His father, Lieutenant General Claire Lee Chennault, was an American military aviator best known for his leadership of the American Flying Tigers, the American flyers publicly recognized for striking a blow against the Japanese military forces only weeks after the Japanese air attack on Pearl Harbor.

His son had flown many combat missions over Europe and, despite his clubfoot, was doing his best to fill his father's shoes by gaining great attention over the range this particular morning. The young pilot was putting on one heck of a display by dropping twenty-five-pound bombs with laser precision in rapid succession from an F-86 Sabre.

Jim, with his instructor and two others, had the best seat in the house, hovering at high altitude while Claire Patterson Chennault performed a training exercise for the upcoming event directly below. Instructor Lockwood called the flights' attention to the exhibition for purposes of seeing and believing.

Jim was doing well in weapons training by staying in the top three of his class based on day-to-day performance. He felt like he had a good handle on things, but after watching young Chennault's performance, he realized he had some room to elevate.

After watching the entire event, this became crystal clear. It was just the motivation he needed to unleash his inner ability.

Capt. Charles C. Carr won that year, in 1954, flying the F-86F. He was a local with the 3595th, TFW, Nellis AFB. Jim made a promise to himself that he would achieve enough status to perform in the Worldwide Gunnery Meet that would eventually become William Tell, the worldwide gunnery meet of United States Air Force Fighter Pilots.

The event was a great highlight to advanced training and an opportunity to watch the top fighter pilots in the world put their talent on display in a competitive environment. It was an amazing spectacle.

From that point forward, Jim approached every training exercise as if he were competing in Gunsmoke, and even though the Korean War had come to an end, he knew he would have other chances at combat, but until then he would approach every practice exercise like war.

War has always existed—it always will—and as a fighter pilot in the United States Air Force, it was now his duty to protect

America by utilizing the skills when needed. Until then, he would keep his skills honed razor-sharp, to use with aggressiveness when the time came. He was nearing the end of the greatest and most advanced training program for fighter pilots in the world, a class taught by heroes—American flying aces. These patriots took their teachings beyond the basics of flying and shooting. They instilled aggression.

"I knew I was under the wings of the greatest group of patriots ever assembled. It doesn't get any better than that," Jim reflected.

> The greatest reward and the basis for all that is to follow, however, is the self-confidence the pilot feels in himself. As this confidence grows, so does his enthusiasm. Enthusiasm increases interest, which in turn pays dividends in over-all accomplishment. All of these qualities together add up to the one thing a training program must produce if the graduate pilots are to be successful in combat – aggressive-ness. It is this pilot aggressiveness which we seek. Without it, all training is useless, for the individual pilot must have the desire to put into effect that which he has been taught. Amazing results have been achieved in combat through aggressiveness alone, but it has been proven time and again that all the training in the world is insufficient when the individual does not have it in his heart to engage the enemy or destroy the target. (Frederick Blesse, *No Guts, No Glory*, iv)

On 25 August 1954, Jim graduated with twenty-three pilots, completing the prescribed course of instruction in advanced flying for the F-86 by finishing the required fifty-four hours in weapons training. Jim as a second lieutenant was assigned to the 366th Fighter-Bomber Wing at Alexandria Air Base in Alexandria, Louisiana, with the 614th Squadron effective 1 September 1954. He was now officially a fighter pilot with Tactical Air Command

(TAC), which consisted of two groupings at the time, each an indication of the type fighter flown and the role they played.

Pilots were distinguished by entering either a fighter day group or fighter-bomber wing. Day fighters were primarily for air-to-air combat (dogfighting). Fighter-bomber pilots were used primarily as air-to-ground in the tactical bombing and ground-attack roles. However, fighter-bombers adapted to other roles when the opportunity arose, particularly dogfighting.

The elements of command in the United States Air Force, in as simple terms as we need mention, starts with the United States Air Force military branch operated out of the Pentagon in Washington, DC. Tactical Air Command (TAC) is a major command organization managed by four-star generals headquartered in Norfolk, Virginia. Strategic Air Command (SAC) is another major command organization managed by four-star generals from their headquarters in Omaha, Nebraska. Twelfth Air Force consists of bases west of the Mississippi River. Ninth Air Force consists of air bases east of the Mississippi River. SAC bases and TAC bases are separate and specialize in their own areas that work as part of the same big overall plan. SAC's main focus in layman's terms is commanding and controlling big bombing with big planes. TAC's focus in simple terms is air defense and tactical air strikes done with fighter jets.

Each air force base is a single wing made of squadrons and consisting of twenty-eight fighter pilots. A wing commander, a director of operations, and a squadron commander for each squadron (in that order) run each air force base. There is also a director of operations under the squadron commander.

The 366th Fighter Bomber Wing at Alexandria Air Base was activated January of 1953. Originally Alexandria Army Air Base, the facility was renamed to England AFB on 23 June 1955.

The wing consisted of the 366th Operational Group (OG) and the 401st Fighter-Bomber Group (FBG). The 366th OG was made up of three operational squadrons (389th, 390th, 391st) equipped, by early 1954, with North American F-86F Sabre jet aircraft, which they would eventually use to the point of having to retire then go back into the predeceasing F-84F until the F-100s arrived. It was a time when USAF fighter pilots flew every day and all day long. It was much, much different than now.

When arriving at the base in Alexandria, Louisiana, Jim reported to the 614th Fighter Bomber Squadron (FBS) under the 401st FBG at Alexandria Air Base. Eventually, the 366th OG would retire, and the 401st FBG would become a wing operating the 612th, 613th, 614th, and 615th squadrons.

It was Jim's first assignment after training, and he again would be working with some of the air force's best. With the war over, he didn't really know what to expect now that it was time to start work, but he knew he was in good company again. Most all the pilots in the 614th had just recently returned from a combat tour in Korea. That was another case of pure fortune for Jim as the youngest pilot in the squadron. "That was okay by me. I was among the very best again and nowhere to go but up with their willingness to guide me," says Jim in the most humble way.

Roger Sprague was one of the first pilots that he met after arriving at Alexandria Air Base and being assigned to the 614th FBS. Jim refers to Roger as a super pilot and flight commander in the 614th FBS when he was still only a green 16 himself, meaning the new pilot in the squadron. They both went to the 612th FBS when that squadron rotated to Chaumont, France, which you'll read about soon. Pilots going to the 612th FBS on that rotation had to be current in the F-86F, which the two of them were.

"Roger became a good friend that I got to fly with many times and still talk too regularly. You might say that we started together and ended together. I met him right away at Alexandria, and you will eventually see that we were some of the last to leave North Vietnam in 1975, two years after the war officially ended in 1973. We left as full colonels, Roger as director of operations, and me as assistant director of operations for the 388th Tactical Fighter Wing (TFW) at Korat Air Base in Thailand," Jim reflects.

For Jim, this was truly the beginning of an exciting fighter pilot career displayed in this book in its true entirety with the help of good records. In the military, you're under constant evaluation, and for officers, every time you finish an assignment or there's a supervisor change, an Officer Effectiveness Report (OER) grades you; there was a constant paper trail following you throughout your career. Upon retiring from the services, Jim received all his military records including all OERs and written reports.

The reports served as a great source of information in putting together his biography, and I will refer to them from time to time going forward. You will see verbatim comments by specific endorsers with dates as you read on.

Initial Report

16 September 1954 – 18 November 1954

Lt. Ryan is considered an above average jet pilot and officer. He seems to be well informed on most phases of his job and shows an eagerness to fly.

This officer willingly accepts additional tasks and assignments, carrying them out to their completion with a minimum of supervision commensurate with his experience. He maintains a neat appearance at all times and is a credit to the Air Force.

This officer exercises good judgment in the economic management of personnel and resources under his supervision, commensurate with his responsibilities. He conforms to the officer code of conduct at all times.

I recommend this officer for continued assignment as a jet fighter pilot.

Robert C. Ruby
USAF, Major
614th, Squadron Commander

Jim was living the dream, but what he expected least was to play a part in a Hollywood motion picture.

It was February 1955, and Hollywood film director Gordon Douglas showed up at England AFB to film part of the Warner Brothers motion picture *The McConnell Story* about Joseph Christopher McConnell Jr., who was the top American flying ace during the Korean War. Captain McConnell was credited with shooting down 16 MiG-15s while flying North American F-86 Sabres with the US Air Force. He was awarded the Distinguished Service Cross and the Silver Star for his actions in aerial combat. McConnell was the first American triple jet-on-jet fighter ace and is still the top-scoring American jet ace.

In 1954, he was temporarily assigned to the service test program for the new F-86H. This was the last and most powerful version of the Sabre and was intended to be a nuclear-capable fighter-bomber. On 25 August 1954, while testing the fifth production F-86H-1-NA (serial number 52-1981) at Edwards Air Force Base, McConnell was killed in a crash following a control malfunction. The cause of the accident was attributed to a missing bolt. Then-major Chuck Yeager was assigned to investigate the crash and replicated the malfunction at a much higher altitude. This height advantage allowed him to safely regain control of the aircraft before it hit the desert floor. The 1955 film *The McConnell Story*, starring Alan Ladd and June Allyson, chronicles his life story.

Jim, as a part of the 614th FBS, would do his part in playing enemy MiG-15 pilots for many scenes, especially one scene involving the rescue of a downed B-29 Superfortress crew that McConnell was trying to protect. Deployed from the 48th Air Rescue Squadron, Eglin AFB, Florida, was a Sikorsky H-19 helicopter used for seven days in February 1955 to work with the 614th FBS, who painted their entire fleet of F-84s communist colors to look like enemy MiGs. They were a grayish blue with red stars on the tail and wings, which caught the attention of many outside of the movie set.

During filming, the Warner Brothers crew dropped the back open on a C-119 flying boxcar to capture close images of the makeshift communist MiGs flown by the 614th. The movie was released on 29 September 1955, and Jim, along with the rest of his squadron, was flown to Hollywood courtesy of Warner Brothers for the premiere party. The film made $3.5 million at the box office.

As the green 16, Jim met many new friends in Alexandria right away. Many of them he'll talk to every week to this day. One longtime friend Jim met in the 614th was his squadron flight commander, John P. Russell, whom everyone knew as Deacon, and then of course, Roger Sprague. Jim tells a story involving both.

It was 1955, a time when America was not at war but flirting with the idea by competing with Russia in a nuclear arms race. Years later, Nikita Khrushchev, the leader of the Soviet Union after the death of Joseph Stalin, quoted himself, saying,

I remember President Kennedy once stated...that the
United States had the nuclear missile capacity to wipe out
the Soviet Union two times over, while the Soviet Union
had enough atomic weapons to wipe out the Unites States
only once... When journalists asked me to comment... I
said jokingly, "Yes, I know what Kennedy claims, and he's
quite right. But I'm not complaining... We're satisfied to
be able to finish off the United States first time round.
Once is quite enough. What good does it do to annihilate
a country twice? We're not bloodthirsty people."

The days of air-to-air combat were antiquated tactics of war.
The air force refocused its strategies around nuclear arms, which
changed the fighting style of fighter pilots. It was a style those
from this era didn't like. They went from training to fight fair and
square against their opponent in the sky while looking them in
the eye from their cockpit to handling nuclear explosives that
could result in the apocalypse.

From a defensive, they were trained to fly low level while hugging peaks and valleys, never breaking five hundred feet from
the ground or five hundred knots in order to evade enemy radar;
this was the low level rule. Low-level routes were put together
by command and sent to headquarters for approval before being
published as official air force record.

Multiple checkpoints were placed throughout the circu-
lar route as designated targets that flights could approach as if
they were in a real attack situation. Eventually, squadrons from
Alexandria would deploy to the hilly and mountainous terrain of
Europe to fly real-time missions using this same low level-flying
tactic. Until then, they would practice on the approved routes
right here in the United States.

One particular day, Jim and Roger were flying a route close
to base, just west of Lake Charles. They were clearly instructed

to stay out of the trees, which were plentiful in the region they were in. Flying just above the tree line was good practice to try and hug the rolling terrain since there were no mountains like in Aviano, Italy.

Jim and Roger were peeling back the tops of a slew of pecan trees in the F-84s when Jim got a bit close for comfort. The tail of his jet ripped through the limbs of a tree, and he soon realized he was having trouble controlling the stick. He fought with it for a while but still managed to get it back to base in one piece.

"I think I hit a bird," said Jim, who I remind you was still green 16 in the 614th.

Roger radioed back, "If you did, he was roosting on the nest."

When they landed and taxied back to the ramp, Jim jumped out to inspect the damage and saw that he had lodged numerous limbs between the back of the fuselage and horizontal tail rudder. It didn't look pretty.

Jim, being the newbie, would have rather ejected at ten thousand feet rather than bring the wounded F-84F back to base, but after debriefing with flight commander Major Deacon Russell, who had a sense of humor, Jim was given a pass due to the nature of the training. Air Force commanders would never go too hard on a pilot for being aggressive. It was still something they instilled despite the change in direction on their new style of fighting tactics. Jim was relieved that he didn't get in trouble but still caught some flak from the others in his squadron, in good fun.

June 21 came, and it was a very special day for Jim when Jeanie gave birth to their first son, Jim Lee Ryan. Jim was not only a squadron fighter pilot, now he was a father, and he embraced the moment for as long as he could. When July rolled around, he was

assigned to the 612th FBS. When walking into the ops building, he ran into—who else—Claire Patterson Chennault, whom
he'd watched compete in Gunsmoke back at Nellis when he was
finishing gunnery school. Chennault, who went by Pat, was the
operations officer of the 612th at the time.

CHANGING SQUADRONS AND PLANES

The 612th FBS would be where Jim met one of the best air-to-air fighter pilots he ever flew with. His name was H. P. Phillips, and he was also the flight commander. Jim would learn a great deal under Phillips—who goes by Hank these days—before they deployed to Chaumont Air Base, France, where a base full of F-86Fs waited.

Building up to the deployment to France, the 612th flew regular practice missions, still utilizing air-to-air combat techniques and readying for the possible chance of engaging with an enemy MiG. Phillips was an air-to-air expert and never gave up the art despite the air force's strategic shift to nuclear contrivances.

"H.P. Phillips was a very soft-spoken guy, but when he strapped into the airplane, he became a tiger," says Jim. Jim, eager to learn, noticed Hank's ability and watched him closely, picking up every tip he could. In Jim's words, "H.P. and I would dogfight in practice, and I couldn't beat him."

Hank said this of Jim: "He was a new pilot when we met, and a very ambitious young man who worked very hard. He was eager to learn."

And learn was what Jim did. When not training at a range or designation in the United States, they performed training exercises overseas to better acclimate to the geography. There were no limits for distance to practice. For instance, they went to a range on Wheelus Air Base in Libya, to further hone their rocket firing, bombing, and strafing skills. Air-to-air gunnery was carried out over a designated area of the Mediterranean Sea, where they fired the Sabre's .50 calibers at a target towed behind a T-33 trainer. Each pilot fired different color dye-dipped bullets to measure results after the exercise, analyzing whose color hit the target panel. It was great practice, yet critical F-86 shooters stayed a certain distance higher, angling off from the tow target and rolling over it right after firing to ensure the .50-caliber bullets went opposite of the training jet. If not, the T-Bird may be inadvertently hit, resulting in a shot-up jet, which did happen at times.

Practice was regular, and Jim was always looking for an opportunity to execute combat air maneuvers. He would look for the chance to jump any potential sparring partner—oftentimes his own flight members—when nothing else was going on. When in Europe, at times, they encountered other planes that were not American or the enemy, but an ally. One day, he engaged with what turned out to be a Canadian pilot in an Mk-6 Sabre, most likely flying out of Zweibrucken Air Base, West Germany. Jim snuck up behind the tailpipe of his brother from the North and aggressively popped out on his wing. He noticed an image painted on the fuselage of the Canadian Sabre that grabbed his attention. "Staring back at me was the cartoon character Yosemite Sam with two six-guns pointing at me," he recalled. "We smiled at each other then moved on. He broke left, and I broke right. It was good fun." In Jim's opinion, the best pilots outside of the United States at the time were Israeli and Canadian.

All this practice would come to good use, with the growing conflict stemming from the outcome of the Second World War and the profound economic and political differences between the

United States and Russia, which still exist despite the dissolution of the Soviet Union in 1991.

*   *   *

At the end of World War II, the Soviets occupied Eastern Europe against the will of those living in the newly acquired areas of the Eastern Bloc, who desired independence and wanted the Soviets out. Between 1945 and 1950, over fifteen million people emigrated from Soviet-occupied eastern European countries to the West. It was a conflicting time and the makings of the North Atlantic Treaty Organization (NATO).

The original twelve nations that signed the North Atlantic Treaty forming NATO in 1949 were Belgium, Canada, Denmark, France, Iceland, Italy, Luxembourg, Netherlands, Norway, Portugal, United Kingdom, and the United States. Collective defense was the result, whereby each member state agreed to mutual defense in response to an attack by any external party. The mobility and striking power of the air force was and is instrumental in furthering the efforts of NATO.

The 401st FBW 612th and 614th Fighter Squadrons were active in the pursuit of NATO objectives from the beginning. Pilots of these two squadrons were checked out and qualified in the F-86 Sabre, as well as the F-84F, and then, eventually, the F-100D Super Sabre.

Jim spent the most time with these two squadrons throughout his career. They were well-respected and participated in numerous firepower demonstrations, tactical exercises, and maneuvers in the United States and, oftentimes, overseas. In mid-1955 through October 1962, there were many occasions where, with little to no advance notice, the tactical fighter squadrons were deployed to bases in Europe and the Middle East in support of NATO as United States Air Force Europe (USAFE).

As the Department of Defense unified command, USAFE, headquartered at Ramstein Air Base in Germany, planned, conducted, controlled, coordinated, and supported air and space operations in Europe, parts of Asia, and Africa to achieve US national and NATO objectives. They trained and equipped US Air Force units pledged to NATO, maintaining combat-ready wings based from Great Britain to Turkey.

In October 1955, Jim, Phillips, Roger Sprague, and Bob Dees—another pilot who lives in Texas who I had the pleasure of meeting—deployed to Chaumont, France, with the 612th on a C-124 Globemaster, a heavy lift cargo aircraft often referred to as Old Shaky by those who flew on them. The 612th unloaded and took over the established base of F-86Fs, replacing the 613th, who boarded the C-124s to return to Alexandria, Louisiana.

As part of the European Tactical Fighter Force once at Chaumont, the 612th rotated to Fürstenfeldbruck Air Base (Fursty) near Munich, the biggest fighter base in Germany during WWII. The base was state-of-the-art, with a fifteen-thousand-foot runway that never froze, despite artic temperatures, due to heated water pipes under it. Jim, only having his wings for a year at this point, was now flying the F-86F over international territory—the biggest assignment he had been part of to date—patrolling the Iron Curtain that divided the free world from the Soviet Union.

From Fursty, it was a five-minute jet ride to the Soviet Bloc nations of East Germany, Czechoslovakia, and Soviet-occupied Austria where the MiG threat was the greatest. The fighter squadron was on Zulu Alert from thirty minutes before sunrise to after sunset, rotating flights inside a twenty-mile-wide barrier zone inside West Germany next to the Soviet-dominated countries. Their mission was to intercept incursions from behind the Iron Curtain by patrolling up and down the border in flights of two or four in constant fashion. If an attack occurred, they were there to engage, but not until calling in permission to fire with (USAFE), who would call the Pentagon for clearance before granting. There was no shortage of rules when in combat.

It was potentially dangerous, but they only found staged threats when radar picked up a group of MiGs moving toward the border high and fast. As they approached, they would turn back and return to base leaving the Cold warriors on Zulu Alert salivating with nothing to engage. This happened multiple times. Even if they had been given the chance, cutting through the red tape for permission to fire would have left them in the same position. It turned out their mere presence was really needed most.

When pilots were not flying the full stretch of the Iron Curtain, they made the best of it by playing quarter-limit poker or frequenting the officers' club for giant African cold-water lobster tails. "The best you've ever tasted and massive in size," said Jim.

One evening, after dinner, they talked the kitchen into letting them have a live one. Sprague had not made it back to his bunk yet, giving Jim and a few other pilots time to pull a prank. They roughed the lobster up a little, making him aggravated and aggressive. Then they put the spiny crustacean at the foot of Sprague's bed, under the covers.

When Sprague returned to the barracks, he headed for his room. He walked past Jim and the guys standing around outside. Sprague, on the verge of slumber from flying the wall before dinner that day and drinking a few scotch on the rocks, said, "Night-night," before entering his room for bed. He was always to bed on time, meeting the air force requirements of eight hours of sleep per night before strapping into a jet the next morning for an exhilarating day.

Ten minutes later, they heard him come unglued with yelling and commotion when he stuck his bare feet in the face of the giant rock lobster. Feeling its long and thick spiny antennas probe his legs in the darkness, he'd thrown the blanket back then quickly turned on the light to inspect.

Jim and the others heard his window creak open and then heard the thud of the lobster as it hit the roof of his car parked just outside of it. The next morning, they discovered it frozen stiff on Sprague's old green Buick. It stayed there for days, proving to be an extended joke at Sprague's expense and coming up in conversation on multiple occasions. Insistent on not giving the pilots more laughs, he played like nothing ever happened and pretended not to notice the frozen lobster. "It was a dirty trick, but a very funny one. The lobster was still there when we left Fursty a few weeks later, our tour of Zulu Patrol ended," said Jim.

After dispersing from Zulu Alert in April of 1956, Jim returned to Chaumont to fly out of the base as part of an additional fighter squadron for USAFE until rotating back to the States with two slight differences. He would return to England AFB in Alexandria as a first lieutenant from a promotion while in France. Alexandria Air Base was renamed to England AFB after John B. England, a squadron commander in the 401st FBG, who was killed in a crash while in Chaumont coincidentally.

Since the job there was ending permanently, they flew the F-86Fs back to England AFB via the North Atlantic Route because the Sabres were not capable of refueling in the air at the time. The reason being they didn't have fueling probes. The Northern Route was an unbelievable experience in the way of navigation. They left France for Prestwick Airport in Scotland then to Reykjavík in Iceland, Bluie West 1 in Greenland, and on to RCAF Station Goose Bay, Labrador, before reaching the States at Presque Isle Airfield in Maine and then going to Langley Field at Virginia before reaching England AFB, Louisiana.

"You can't imagine how cold ice and snow is until you've been that route. It's the only way to go due to the need for refueling on land every couple of hours or so. I remember a couple of those stops. Snow was over twenty feet deep," said Jim.

When returning from France, Jim took some leave time to go and pick up his wife and child, who were staying with his parents in Lyons, Kansas, since he was away in Europe often. He had built up $7,000 in poker winnings from playing quarter-limit poker with other pilots during downtime in Europe.

Jim called his mother, who was still working at the Oldsmobile dealership, to let her know he was coming. He asked her to get a new Super Eighty-Eight model Olds in makeready and told her that he was coming to pick it up along with Jeanie and Jim Lee to take back to Louisiana.

He rented a home for them in Alexandria and made arrangements through another pilot's family, who owned a furniture store nearby to furnish the house. Life had come a long ways since Eastern Oklahoma, where he grew up as kid. He had his family together, a new car in front of a fully furnished house, as well as $2,000 extra in the bank—all paid for by poker winnings while in Europe. I guess the harder you work, the luckier you get. "I haven't ever gone without money in the bank since then." Jim smiles.

After arriving back to work at England AFB, the 612th flew the F-86s on to Sacramento, California, and turned them into the storage aircraft boneyard there—a place where outdated aircraft go. Dees recalls the flight back from Chaumont. They were all in formation when one of the pilots came up lost. Flying in thick weather with poor visibility, he heard the flight leader calling for one of the pilots who was out of sight. After a little time passed, the missing pilot responded by saying he'd looked down to light a cigarette, and when he'd looked up, they were gone. It took him a little while to join up again. Dees remembers, "He was in big trouble when we landed, not only for smoking in the cockpit but for breaking formation."

With the F-86s gone, the 612th, 613th, and 614th of the 401st FBW was asked to recheck in its predecessor, the F-84F, which was a less sophisticated aircraft. The good news was there was a new plane due to arrive in June of 1957. Jim checked out in the North American F-100D Super Sabre on 29 July 1957. It was single-seat fighter-bomber with more advanced avionics, larger wings, tail fin, and landing flaps than its forerunners. The F-100 was the first USAF fighter capable of supersonic speed in level flight—864 miles per hour or Mach 1.3—making it a Super Sabre. The plane was armed with four 20 mm Pontiac M39A1 revolver cannons and could carry a wide range of conventional bombs and missiles as well as Mark 7, MK 28, MK 38, and MK 43 specialty bombs (nuclear). The avionics were state of the art, with autopilot, a low-altitude bombing system, and a rearward radar warning. With the evolving aircraft came the onset of the way fighter pilots were asked to fight. Nuclear weapons were now the focus, which required a different way of flying. Low-altitude missions were becoming more of a measure. The days of dogfighting were slowly moving to more of a memory at this point, being taught with less and less emphasis.

The new jet was state of the art—the best—but some of the other tools used by fighter pilots at the time were not so much. In fact, one particular thing was despised. Survival suits were developed for pilots to wear when flying over large bodies of water with dangerously low temperatures. Should a fighter pilot have to eject, the suit was designed to increase their chances of survival in otherwise near-fatal water temperatures. They were made out of a very thick rubber material with a diagonal zipper from the chest to lower abdomen used to put the suit on, and another in the groin area for purposes of handling the call of nature. Under the cumbersome rubber suit, a G-suit was worn, and then an inflatable Mae West (life vest) around the neck to top it off. Ocean crossings were anywhere between ten to twelve hours, sometimes nonstop. Jim recalls one time flying seventeen hours straight without stepping out of the cockpit.

The suit had a tube connected for purposes of attaching the plane's air-conditioning. The groin zipper used to pee was useless since a large rubber sleeve had to be rolled out once unzipped measuring twelve inches in length. You can see why it was pointless.

Fighter pilots have a macho reputation, but not many men are that well-endowed. Even if you were a freak of nature, you may never have the chance to unzip in transit. In which case, you simply pee in the watertight suit—the most popular choice. Once landing, take the damn thing off and give it to maintenance for a good hose down.

Now that we know how number one was handled in flight, what about number two? The pilots called the suits poopy suits, but don't let the name fool you. Jim said few did that in them because of crew conditioning.

Days before a long-distance ocean crossing, the flight would undergo a preparatory phase called crew conditioning, where professional staff regulated diet and sleep patterns. Diet consisted of two meals per day made of high protein, low-residue food. Military physicians prescribed sleep medication at bedtime and stimulants in the very early morning to change the biological clock for bowel movement. Once in flight, pilots depended on two canteens connected to drinking tubes stored behind the hard narrow seat of the F-100 to hydrate. Also within reach was a small storage compartment for low-residue sandwich bites for food.

Despite the poopy suit's nickname, it served dual purpose of surviving cold-water temperatures, but more often, peeing in when not having any other choice while in flight.

The suit, as unpopular as it was, served a purpose when flying long distances while relying only on midair refueling. The Mid-Atlantic route to Europe was this type of ocean crossing, departing from the States out of Myrtle Beach, South Carolina, most often to Libya, Morocco, Turkey, Spain, Italy, France, and Germany. Sometimes, they would stop off in the Azores, an island with a long runway and all the facilities of a standard air force base.

"From 1955 to 1962, I flew across the ocean seventeen times, so many it was as familiar to me as going to work in the morning. I had a few problems along the way, such as running out of fuel, a fire warning light that continuously malfunctioned, as well as loosing other aircraft systems. Fortunately, I made it out in each instance and lived to talk about it today. I wish I could say that for everyone flying the same route, but sadly, I can't. We had aircraft and pilot losses along the way, but those guys are okay. They just flew on ahead to fighter-pilot heaven. The rest of us are in trail west and closing fast to the reunion of all reunions. Amen," says Jim.

Jim bringing the first A-7D Corsair into
Davis Monthan AFB for the 40th TFS.

Jim standing on the ramp at Davis Monthan AFB
when in the process of organizing the 40th TFS.

The 358th Lobos under commander Jim Ryan at Davis Monthan AFB.

Jim receiving a cold Budweiser from the director of
operations at Myrtle Beach AFB in South Carolina after
leading the entire 358th TFS there on an exercise.

Jim flying an A7-D while the ops officer for the 40th TFS.
Photographer of the 11th Tactical Drone Squadron who
shared a building with the 40th TFS took the photo.

Colonel Archie Hyle, commander of the 1st Cavalry's 1st Brigade
playing quick draw with Jim who took the photo in Vietnam, 1966.

Jim in pilot training at Webb AFB in early 1954.
He was boarding a T-33 trainer jet.

Jim climbing into a T-6 Texan before an hour and a half
flight during primary training in Moultrie, Georgia.

Jim as an Aviation Cadet Col. in 1954 just before
graduating the program in Big Spring, Texas.

Col. Jim Ryan on July 10, 2014 in Dayton, Ohio, at a
wounded warrior event. Photo taken by Tommy Meyer.

Jim in An Khe, Vietnam in 1966 standing in front
of his O-1 Bird Dog holding his AK-47.

Jim took the photo of a teenage boy who was captured by the
1st Brigade during Operation IRVING in Vietnam.

Jim when starting the control tower operator course.

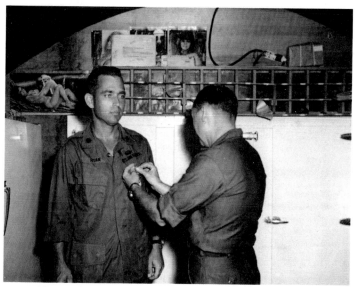

Jim receives a Distinguished Flying Cross, late 1966 in An Khe, Vietnam, for flying the UH-1D helicopter in combat.

Jim's father Ernest with youngest son Tony in Westport,
Washington, 1963. Ernest is holding King Salmon.

Fourth from the right is Jim after delivering one of three F-100Fs
to the Danish Air Force at Karup AB, Denmark in 1962. Third
from the left is Skip Carlson and right of him is Jim (White Fang)
Hartney. Far left is the State Minister of Denmark, Jens Otto Krag.

Jim in the cockpit of an F-111D at Nellis AFB, Las Vegas, Nevada, in 1975 as Chief of Safety for the Twelfth Air Force.

Jim is fourth from the left at Fürstenfeldbruck near Munich, Germany, 1955 while patrolling the Iron Curtain.

Snow covered F-86 Sabre's on the line at Fürstenfeldbruck,
Germany, during Zulu Patrol in December 1955.

Twelfth Air Force Commander, General Hughes presenting Jim with
a medal at a dinner party held at Bergstrom AFB in Austin, Texas,
immediately after he returned from his last tour in Vietnam, 1975.

The house the FAC's built in Vietnam, 1966.

Left is Jeanie Ryan with Jim's mother Faye.

Jeanie Ryan at her home in Lyons, Kansas in 1952.

Left is Charlie Johnson with Jim after a flight in
1953 during Aviation Cadet Pilot Training.

Left is Charlie Johnson with Jim during Aviation Cadet Pilot Training.

Jim receives notification of his selection as Forward Air Controller
with the U.S. Army by a personal letter from Gen. Curtis E.
LeMay, Air Force chief of staff. Gen. Walter Sweeney Jr., Tactical
Air Command commander, presented the letter to him.

Left is Jim speaking with James Jabara (center) with a
German student pilot on the right at Luke AFB.

Second from left is Jim with James Jabara (third from left)
and two German student pilots in the back of a ramp truck
on their way to their F-104s waiting on the ramp.

Second from left is Jim next to James Jabara (smoking cigar)
and two German Luftwaffe student pilots in the back of a ramp
truck on their way to their F-104 Starfighters' at Luke AFB.

James Jabara center speaking to Jim on the left with a
German student pilot on the right at Luke AFB.

Jim at home on leave with Jeanie, and about to take a
new Super Eighty-Eight Olds for a drive in 1953.

Left is 10-yr.-old Jim Lee with five-yr.-old
brother Tony at Luke AFB in 1965.

Second from left on the back row is Jim next to BB Huffman third from left. The rest of the back row is instructors, and the German students are on the front row at Luke AFB.

Jim with other 1st Brigade soldiers north of An Khe in the Binh Dinh Province during a coastal sweep mission in Vietnam, 1966.

Jim sitting in the back of the commanders chopper he's
piloting, taking a break before pressing on with a coastal
sweep mission in search of the enemy in 1966.

Jim in steaming hot Vietnam, July 1966, it was 115 degrees outside.

Jim holding a monkey at a permanent 1st Brigade Battalion camp right after he arrived at the War. Ammunition boxes are stacked to his left.

Jim standing at the edge of a jungle mountain area during Operation IRVING after a strike shown in the distance.

Near the finish of Aviation Cadet Pilot Training at Webb
AFB in 1954. From the left are Jim Ryan, Lt. John C.
Wilhite, Haakon A. Lunde and Duane D. Cook.

Jim and Jeanie married in Lyons, Kansas, on 30 May 1954 only
four days after completing Aviation Cadet Pilot Training and
earning his wings, and receiving his commission as 2nd Lt.

The photo taken before William Tell in 1962 that was used for the program. Jim attended as an alternate for the 401st TFW.

HIGH FLIGHT
By John Gillespie Magee, Jr.

Oh, I have slipped the surly bonds of earth
And danced the skies on laughter-silvered wings;
Sunward I've climbed, and joined the tumbling mirth
Of sun-split clouds—and done a hundred things
You have not dreamed of—wheeled and soared and swung
High in the sunlit silence. Hov'ring there,
I've chased the shouting wind along, and flung
My eager craft through footless halls of air.
Up, up the long, delirious, burning blue
I've topped the windswept heights with easy grace
Where never lark, or even eagle flew.
And, while with silent, lifting mind I've trod
The high untrespassed sanctity of space,
Put out my hand, and touched the face of God.

High Flight by John Gillespie Magee, Jr.

OCEAN CROSSING

Jim flew the Mid-Atlantic Route several times, but there is one time he remembers most. In September 1958, he, Sprague, Russell, and five others were part of an ocean crossing assignment with the 612th TFS. The flight of eight, F-100Ds, filed their flight plan at England AFB to deploy to Myrtle Beach in South Carolina, then to Europe via the Mid-Atlantic Route. Scheduled refueling was always critical when taking this path over the Bermuda Triangle through the Azores, where no alternate route existed. Roughly a ten-hour flight to Nouasseur Air Base near Casablanca, French Morocco, the flight would have to rendezvous for refueling approximately every two to three hours. Out of Myrtle Beach, the first airborne refueling spot was over Bermuda, with the second between the drop-off point ninety miles east and a checkpoint called Ocean Station Echo, which is a large seafaring vessel continually on station in the middle of the Atlantic. From there, the flight was nonstop until landing at Lajes AB on Terceira—a central Azorean island—to refuel for a third time, then nonstop to Morocco in North Africa.

During this crossing, the flight reached Ocean Station Echo, where they joined up with their second set of tankers for fuel. After twelve minutes passed, the F-100s started dropping off of their lines, but Jim wasn't taking on fuel as quickly as the others due to a malfunction. He radioed he was still short 1,800 pounds to the flight leader, who told him to go ahead and drop off. They were close enough to the Azores to get there on the amount of fuel he had. Against his better judgment, Jim dropped off, which proved to be a near life-threatening mistake later.

After dropping off, they were informed by the lead tanker pilot of a new weather forecast for the Azores region at their arrival. Unexpectedly, it included low overcast, heavy rain, high wind, and thirty-foot ocean swells around the island. Major Johnson, leading the flight of eight, cut the heading they were given to Terceira in half, suspect of the strong headwind, as well as the drastic difference in what they had been flying up to this point. What he didn't expect was an active volcano on the island of Faial, a small western Azorean Island encompassing the city of Horta, which was releasing magnetic ash into the air and causing all kinds of navigation problems. Dialing a beacon into the navigation system of the F-100, along with a certain amount of self-computing by the pilot, typically gave an exact heading for landing. The Horta beacon they were attempting to use turned out to be useless.

Jim was flying wing position on the far-right side, number four in the second flight of four. Since leaving the tankers, they had cruise climbed to forty-five thousand feet and were smothered by the weather in close formation. Timewise, they had to be near Lajes Field, doing fuel checks regularly. "That's when I realized I had approximately 2,500 pounds less than the rest of the flight," Jim said. They began discussing what they were going to do if they didn't find the landing field very shortly.

Cruising at approximately 3,000 pounds of fuel per hour gave them under an hour at the altitude they were flying. Jim had much less. He advised the flight that he would stay with the flight until reaching 500 pounds then shut his engine down, staying close on the same heading and altitude to ensure close proximity if they popped out of the weather before he did.

"If I popped out first, I could advise them of any observation I noticed, like light from ships or land. Remembering the weather report for Lajes was low overcast, rain, and sea swells running approximately thirty feet, no matter how you look at it, we were all in deep trouble if we didn't find the field in the next few minutes," Jim stated.

Inevitably, he hit the 500 lb. fuel marker and put the plan into execution.

He said, "Guys, I'm below 500 pounds of fuel. I'll shut it down, keep the same heading and altitude, so let me know if you break out, then I'll follow you. Otherwise, I need to conserve fuel to gain as much time as possible in my descent. Unless the weather lifts, at five thousand feet, I'll have to eject into the ocean, and you should have a good idea where I'm at to direct the search for me."

Lead, with no other choice, agreed. "That sounds like the best plan, Jim. You hang in there, and we'll find our way out of this." Just as lead finished his sentence, another pilot in the flight by the name of Bear Hasty chimed in. He said, "Jim, I don't think we need to leave you behind, I'll fall back with you until the rest find our runway." He wouldn't agree to that and asked Bear to go ahead with the others. It was a moment of solitude. They all knew it wasn't a good situation, and the chances of Jim making it were next to none. They also knew that even though they had more fuel, they were still at high risk themselves.

Being a thousand miles from nowhere, chances were they would all wind up ejecting into the Atlantic, in which case the thirty-foot swells would probably engulf them all.

The one calculation Jim held on to was the fact that the others had 2,500 pounds of fuel as planned. With that, he knew if their heading was correct going in—the same heading lead adjusted—that should put them in the vicinity. If the adjustment was off, they were in trouble.

Just before Jim idled back, he suddenly saw number three man's wingtip, which hadn't been visible before. "At that very moment, we all broke out of the clouds. The sky was getting dark, but I could see all seven of the other aircraft in our flight. I immediately rolled inverted to look down," says Jim.

The instant he rolled his plane over to get a better look at what was below, he miraculously noticed a compact vertical hole through the weather. It was approximately one mile wide in circumference. At the bottom, he saw part of a runway. Quickly, he did a split-S dive, a descending half loop that put him in level flight the exact opposite direction at a lower altitude. Now idling, he turned the nose of the F-100 down, tightly spiraling like a dart into the opening of the clouds. At all costs, he had to keep the runway in sight.

Ironically, the split S is taught to be used in dogfighting as a maneuver used by a pilot to lose an enemy in an air-to-air battle. Jim said, "If you can lure your opponent in behind where he thinks he is about to nail you, then split S dive as close to the ground as you know you can recover without crashing. The enemy, who is concentrating more on killing you than watching where he is going, will try to follow. Once the nose of his plane gets down, he can't possibly recover from his position. He will crash and die, which counts as a kill for you."

The fact that Jim used this maneuver in this situation is poetic. They were not dogfighting against an enemy aircraft but rather against mother nature, who was tight on their tail.

Deep into the hole, he kept his spiral gripped tight, careful to stay within the clearing, not straying from his only visible passage to safety. Slowly coming into sight below was a quarter of the runway adjacent to the ocean. He had landed on Lajes Air Base often enough; there was no mistaking it. Jim could only hope he was right since he had laid it all on the line in an instant. "I've got it," he radioed to the others.

He heard lead instruct the rest of the flight to follow him down and stay as close as possible without losing sight of him. Sprague was the first one in behind Jim. The rest followed suit one by one in spiraling formation.

"I put out my speed brakes using all the rudder I could to keep the runway visible. Numerous times, it started to fade out because of the deteriorating weather conditions, but somehow, I managed to keep my eyes on it," Jim remembers.

With the overcast, rain, and darkness coming on fast, it was becoming more and more of a challenge. If he lost it at any one point, there was zero chance of recovery. The same went for the others behind him.

"Just when I thought I was going to give it all up, I suddenly broke out and was over the center of the runway at about a thousand feet. I sucked that big Hun around to a downwind leg, put the gear down, and made a great landing, not knowing if I landed with or against the wind. And it didn't make a damn bit of difference at this point. I was on the runway doing fine, and nothing else mattered," said Jim.

Using the full twelve-thousand-foot distance of the runway, he activated his drag chute to slow the tired jet, and at the very end of the strip, dropped the chute off in the holding area, then turned the Hun around to wait for the others. He opened the canopy so he could see, looking and waiting while listening over the radio.

Suddenly, he saw seven sets of landing lights glide in at the opposite end of the runway, touching down one at a time with little distance between them.

Jim reflects, "At that moment, I felt the rain begin to fall, so I closed the canopy. As I did, the opening in the sky closed within seconds of the last jet landing. The overcast became so heavy I could barely see them on the runway, but by counting, I knew they were all there. You can't imagine what a relief that was."

As they turned off at the end of the runway, passing in front of him one by one, reality sat in. It was as picturesque as a slow-motion movie scene, each pilot giving him a wave or a thumbs-up.

What happened next was even more chilling. As the seven other pilots went by Jim, he said, "I'm so glad to see you guys down here with me. Go ahead, and I'll follow behind you." Together again, they started rolling one behind the other to the ramp. Jim pushed his throttle up to follow suit. The throttle he hadn't touched since pulling it to idle after rolling inverted at forty-five thousand feet was nonresponsive. The jet didn't move. He was completely out of fuel, and the engine had flamed out somewhere on the way down. "I never used the throttle during the descent or landing," he humbly said.

Base personnel came out to give Jim a tug back to the ramp where all eight planes were left for the night to maintenance and prepare for flight into Europe the next morning.

"At best I can remember, we all hugged, then the eight of us boarded a bus to head straight to the officers' club for a drink and dinner before returning to our quarters that evening," said

Jim. "What happened in 1958 seems like it was only yesterday. I would like to ask the reader, what you think got us through this flight? I certainly know, do you? It wasn't completely skill and definitely not us getting lucky. Everything throughout this occurrence hinged on constant observation, staying omnipresent with split-second decisions being made in rapid succession—all the time with heavy consequence. This has to do with living in the now while having faith. It was divine intervention, which is the same thing that has stayed with me so many times throughout my life. Pay close attention to the rest of my story, and you'll see it over and over."

What looked like a catastrophe turned out to be a successful mission. "Every one of the pilots I was flying with that evening was a phenomenal fighter pilot, and we made it thanks to the good Lord and our flying ability," Jim said with glassy eyes.

Through all the excitement and concentration of getting from forty-five thousand feet of darkness to the runway, he didn't realize his engine had flamed out. Through experience, he knew he had plenty of airspeed from the vertical dive to get the plane on the ground. Whether the engine was running or not wasn't an immediate problem, but holding a tight position in the high-speed dive through the small opening in the clouds to get to the runway was. Through the last ten minutes, he had gone from certain death to safe on the ground with a can-do attitude and some help.

CREW CHIEFS AND COMMANDERS

Fighter pilots are assigned a crew chief to take care of their aircraft. Jim's crew chief while at England AFB was one who became a lifelong friend, Bobby Jones. Every crew chief takes great pride in caring for the plane of their pilot. In fact, painted on the side of every fighter jet is the name of the pilot and crew chief. They spend their careers taking care of planes they don't personally get to fly in themselves—ever—unless there's an unordinary circumstance. Jim made sure Jones got to experience their plane in the air. He got special permission from wing commander and Colonel Frank "Speedy Pete" Everest to take Jones with him to deliver an F-100D for static display at a special air force event in Arkansas.

On their way home, a couple days later, they flew over Jones's hometown in Mississippi to maybe see his family waiting to wave from the front porch. On arrival, they dropped to the appropriate altitude in order to recognize the small town. Jim pointed it out to Jones. "There it is," he said.

"That's not it, Jim, not it," said his crew chief.

Jim answered laughingly, "It sure is. Give me a checkpoint, and I'll prove it."

Jones said, "There was a water tower in the yard of the high school."

"Got it. That's it," Jim said.

"No, it's not," said Jones, confused.

Crew chiefs are the best aircraft mechanics the air force has to offer, but navigation or, more specifically, trying to spot something on the ground at high altitude moving fast isn't something they're used to. Jim, knowing that, patiently told Jones to put his face close to the canopy on the left, and he would take him down closer to make sure he could see well enough. So Jones did. Jim plunged the Super Sabre to lower altitude at over four hundred miles per hour, as if he were flying a wartime sortie. Jones's face was stuck to the glass like a suction cup. "That's it, that's it!" he yelled with affirmation.

"I know it is," said Jim. "Now where is your house from here?"

Jones answered, "Just across the river to the east a couple of miles." By the time he finished his sentence, they were a mile past the river, now climbing. Once Jones had his visual bearings, he told Jim, "There it is on the right! See all the people out front?"

Upon nearing the house, Jim nosed down into a whifferdill turn from the front to give his crew chief a bird's-eye view quickly. Grabbing for his camera to take a picture, Jones made close eye contact with his wife through the viewfinder. As he attempted to wave with his free hand, Jim pulled the nose up, thrusting into a steep climb that made the scariest roller coaster look like a kiddie ride. The high positive G-force jerked Jones's head down uncontrollably, and he dropped the camera without ever snapping a photo. Jim climbed to the top of the loop, and Jones's chin dug into his chest. "Jim, I dropped my camera, and I can't lift my head up," he muttered. Mounting the top of the loop to plunge earthbound again, Jones briefly regained control enough to wave at his family, who were walking around in the front yard in amazement. Jim rolled the F-100 out to head for Alexandria, rocking the wings from side to side as a wave good-bye.

His crew chief gained great satisfaction in the way the F-100 performed that day, and he let it be known that he was especially proud to see firsthand how Jim was able to operate it to full potential. Knowing the United States had very capable pilots like Jim sitting on alert in Europe brought some peace of mind to him during a time wherein many Americans were in fear of a nuclear holocaust.

Europe was becoming more of a growing concern due to Soviet Premier Nikita Khrushchev issuing an ultimatum to Western powers by giving them six months to agree to withdraw from Berlin. The United States, United Kingdom, and France responded firmly by asserting their determination to remain in West Berlin and to maintain their legal right of free access to that city.

The world's superpowers were at odds, and no one really knew what the outcome would be. As a US fighter pilot during this era, Jim was part of a group that stayed in a constant state of readiness to deploy anywhere at any time if and when needed. Most of the time, USAFE kept a good rotation of pilots in close reach for ease of convenience. TDY assignments were anywhere from three to nine months, sometimes with only a minute's notice. In this case, Jim packed and left without being able to let anyone know where he was going, including his wife. His family wouldn't know when he might return. After a couple days, air force personnel would contact the family with more details. Jim always wrote right away too, spelling out what he could.

In Jeanie Ryan's words,

> There was strict instruction for the wives of pilots to keep
> confidential. We were not told where they were going, and

we were not to ask or tell. If someone asked us where they were, even close family, we simply smiled and changed the subject. It was a scary time in the world, and not having him home with the boys and me was difficult. Most of the time, I stayed with Jim's parents in Kansas through those years. I always worried about him and tried not to watch the news or read about it, which would make it worse. Being with his mom and dad helped, we kept each other encouraged.

Some things were never spoken of due to security reasons. During many of the years Jim was TDY in Europe, he was sitting nuclear alert. For Jim, this stint began in Bitburg, Germany, in late 1957 then in Aviano, Italy, through early 1960, for rising concern of Russian threats. Jim had been given more responsibility as a nuclear weapons instructor, something he didn't particularly like at the time. It was especially disappointing for fighter pilots who enjoyed the challenge of air-to-air combat but now had to train for use of nuclear weapons.

Four F-100Ds sat waiting near a runway near Rivolto AFB, Codroipo, Italy, and province of Udine. Only a few yards from the ramp sat a vault which contained four nuclear weapons, Mark 7 American nuclear bombs, and Mark 12s locked tight behind security.

The Mark 7 "Thor" was the first tactical nuclear bomb adopted by US Armed Forces. It was also the first weapon to be delivered using the toss method with the help of the low-altitude bombing system (LABS). The ball-shaped power source, the size of a bowling ball, was uranium 235 securely locked in the center of the weapon when armed. The Mark 7 required a rubber-gloved hands-on approach when arming and disarming. When dropped correctly, an implosion squeeze activated the uranium causing an explosion no one can fathom. The Mark 7 was in service from

1952 to 1968, with 1,700–1,800 having been built. Few people had ever seen one, much less touched one, until they became museum pieces over the last seven years.

The Mark-12 was notable for being significantly smaller in size and weight compared to prior implosion-type nuclear weapons. For example, the overall diameter was only twenty-two inches, compared to the immediately prior Mark-7 which had a thirty-inch diameter, and the volume of the implosion assembly was only 40 percent the size of the Mark-7's. It was more automated than the Mark 7, using a spherical implosion assembly, levitated pit, and 92-point detonation. Manufactured by the United States of America starting in 1954, it saw service until 1962.

Nicknamed Brok, there were only 250 produced.

Four nuclear alert teams rotated regularly through primary, secondary, standby, and alert status. There were three men to a team—a crew chief, fighter pilot, and weapons armor—and they had specific duties including waking their nuke up, arming it, and loading it on the team's fully fueled plane. At night, they put their nuke back to bed by disarming it safely in the vault. Each team had to pass by security in order to approach the hangared F-100s. If a team approached the gate missing any one of the team members, security had clearance to shoot and kill the possible intruders. Each team member was given a code word to alarm security with in a crisis situation. For example, if an imposter had a member at gunpoint from behind, the guard would recognize the code and head off the possible encroachment.

If a team was asked to drop a nuclear weapon, this could result in a one-way flight for the pilot. They were trained to drop the bomb then get as far away as possible to eject from the plane when out of fuel. The best place would be near a body of water or in hilly terrain where cover exists. Once on the ground, dig a hole like a cave, crawl in, and pull the dirt, rocks, and solid debris in behind for protection. Then don't come out for forty-eight hours for the best chance of avoiding nuclear fallout.

Jim remembers a few close calls to take the runway loaded with a live nuclear weapon, but never getting the orders to leave the ground; it was more of a test. "I'm glad we never had to drop one," he said. "The thought of not having any more fuel than what you had and no airbase to land on after a drop meant it was a one-way trip probably, but it was what we were asked to do." Danger was part of the job, and they lived with it every day.

For example, twenty-four aircraft left the runway on a zero-notice deployment over the Mid-Atlantic, stopping in Wethersfield AFB in England (the UK) then on to Spangdahlem AB in Germany. They were carrying 450-gallon external fuel tanks to further fueling capacity into Wethersfield. When arriving at Wethersfield late, they filled internal tanks only for the short flight to Spangdahlem the next morning. "The 450-gallon external tanks were troublesome for their weight when full. If empty, they could be dangerous due to elusive overflow from the internal tanks after sitting through the night," said Jim. At times, full internal tanks sitting overnight would feed fuel lines, seeping into the external tanks. Before taking off, pilots were instructed to activate their fuel pumps to make sure the 450s were completely empty. Otherwise, fuel that overflowed sloshed back and forth on takeoff, putting the F-100 in a possible nose-high position. The result was the deadly Sabre dance.

The first flight of four out of Wethersfield would be a reminder of the danger involved and the Sabre dance. Upon takeoff, Jim was flying in the number three position behind John Wagnon. In number two position was Gale Kerr, who unexpectedly took off first behind lead, who'd aborted because of a maintenance issue.

Less fortunate, Wagnon took off behind Kerr. His external tanks took on fuel through the night—and evidently, a great deal of it. Splashing back and forth, it set the Sabre off balance. On takeoff, the Hun's nose lifted, taking Wagnon into the dreaded dance. The twenty-eight-thousand-pound jet rolled up and out of control, partially airborne directly over the nuclear alert area before crashing into flames. The pilots sitting alert in the shack near the ramp and runway witnessed the whole thing, barely escaping death themselves. Jim left the runway behind Wagnon, who was on the ground in flames. "I saw his face at close distance as he rolled and inverted, just seconds before he went down. I had to go ahead with my takeoff," remembers Jim. It was reminder of the consequences of not making certain external tanks were completely empty before takeoff.

Jim just made captain and was on his way back to England AFB for some good news—his second son was born. Tony Ryan came into the world on March 5, 1960. His family was growing, along with his responsibilities as a fighter pilot, and his time at England AFB was nearing expiration. Gaining more and more experience, he had earned the respect of Wing Commander Everest who always called him for a favor he was glad to do. He didn't want to leave the 401st just yet.

While Jim was home on leave in Lyons, Kansas, celebrating his new son with family, Everest called with a favor. He sent a T-33 to Hutchison, which was thirty-five miles away from Lyons, to pick up Jim and take him to Sacramento, California. "There, you will meet up with two other pilots, Spike Carlson and Jim Hartney, to pick up three new F-100Fs (two-seaters). Sign for them and take the aircraft to Myrtle Beach to deploy to Châteauroux AFB and then to Karup AB in Denmark. When you get there, leave the three fighters with the Royal Danish Air Force," said Everest.

"I want you to stay there for twenty-one days to finish the assignment, doing whatever you can to keep you busy. That will give you a new overseas return date, and I can meet the requirements to keep you in the wing. I want to keep you with me," he said.

"We drank the best red wine and ate our share of escargot all over Europe waiting for those twenty-one days to end," Jim said. It was a demanding job with the occasional perk, and sometimes, you had to do things in order to work around the system and stay where you wanted. In this case, it was an enjoyable work-around.

On another occasion, to Jim's surprise, Everest asked him to fly his wing from Myrtle Beach to Wheelus AFB in North Africa, only the two of them. In North Africa, they would meet up with world-famous test pilot, Chuck Yeager, coming in from Spain. Close friends, Everest and Yeager would go on together to Aviano, Italy, for other air force business. Inseparable, the two test pilots had been given the toughest, most dangerous assignments for the air force because of their daring talent, and they had become very close friends through it all. The two were Mavericks who brought great publicity to the USAF and lived between the rules, never being questioned much by command. After glorious years as test pilots, they became commanders and eventually general officers. Yeager was a squadron commander of the 417th Fighter-Bomber squadron under the 50th FBW in Toul-Rosiere, France. As you know, Everest was wing commander of the 401st TFW in Alexandria, Louisiana, and later went on to work at the Pentagon in Washington, DC, during the same time Jim would work there.

"Those two guys were some of the toughest guys I've been around, and I've been around some tough guys. I only met Yeager a few times, but I worked closely with Everest," said Jim. They worked hard for the air force and played hard with few questions asked. Not that this happened, but it could have, and if it did happen, it happened like this. Yeager and Everest could have been questioned one night by a provost marshal after a menial incident outside a nightclub in Europe. They were somewhat offended by being questioned, knowing that they were in the right decided to put the PM in time-out. So they locked the marshal up in his own jail for the night and let him think about it until the next morning. The air force was good to Everest and Yeager, and they were a good draw for the air force. Regardless of their skylarking, everyone loved them. "They were fighter pilot heroes, some of the very best," said Jim.

This was a time when the air force needed the best. Berlin continued as a growing point of confrontation, and finally, during the early months of 1961, the East German government actively sought a means of halting the emigration of its population to the West. By spring they procured and stockpiled building materials for the erection of the Berlin Wall. The East German army began to close the border, and by morning, on Sunday August 13, 1961, the border to West Berlin had been shut.

During the Berlin Crisis (approximately September 1961), the 614th was deployed to Ramstein Air Base, Germany, to support the West Germans. Short a pilot, they took Jim from the 612th to participate in the operation. Jim was not only rising in rank, he was developing a reputation as a top gun by winning an intrasquadron high-altitude bombing competition with a score so low that it caught the entire wing's attention. He was known for dropping fifty consecutive bombs on bull's-eyes during one of these competitions, unprecedented. The 401st TFW had a reputation for performing the best firepower demonstrations for the USAF's most elite generals, and Jim was a big part of those showings. He was also an assistant nuclear weapons officer, which made him a special asset, considering the objective of the upcoming mission.

At the initial briefing, the 614th personnel were informed that due to the close proximity of the USSR, if an Intercontinental Ballistic Missile (ICBM) were to be launched, they would have only thirty minutes to launch the 614th aircraft and retire to the nearest German bunker. An (ICBM) is a ballistic missile with a minimum range of more than 3,400 miles typically designed for nuclear weapons delivery.

The 614th flew nonstop out of Alexandria to Ramstein AB, Germany, the frontline NATO base during the Cold War. USAFE kept fighter pilots in F-100s and the new F-104 Starfighter—a single-engine, high-performance supersonic interceptor aircraft—flying up and down the wall twenty-four hours a day, on alert and fully armed with GAR-8 warhead missiles. They were told not to fly into Berlin, where enemy Russian MiGs were active. However, they were permitted to engage the enemy if they crossed the border by giving the international signal to drop their landing gear and take it down immediately or else.

USAFE put C-130 aircraft in the air to fly the corridors against the Soviet ultimatum even after threats were made. If a flight of MiGs would have approached, American F-100s would have been there to answer, but they never had to.

There was too much to risk, and if there had been a firefight, it would have surely caused world conflict. Both USAFE and Russian pilots knew this. There was more flirting than anything else during Jim's involvement in the crisis.

DOC RYAN AND WILLIAM TELL

Not long after flying the Berlin Wall, Jim was again put on nuclear alert in Turkey, where he earned a new nickname derived from a happening that had nothing to do with flying. When his group ran into some much-deserved downtime, being the constant adventurers they were, they put together a little R & R trip into the mountains of Northern Turkey.

When flying over the Aryan Mountains in Turkey—the same mountain region where Noah docked his ark—Jim's flight couldn't help but notice a beautiful blue water hole perfectly positioned in the most pristine setting on the southern slope of the mountains.

The group of fighter pilots, along with enlisted personnel, got approval to load up a truck full of supplies and drive into the rough terrain. They brought a translator to help communicate when passing through various villages on their way to find the majestic blue hole they spotted while flying.

Out of Incirlik AFB, they took out on a 250-mile journey through the high mountains in search of the spot. They wandered down the narrow dirt roads and through the rough terrain, occasionally coming upon a village. Each one looked like it belonged to eighteenth century Native Americans. They were nothing more than tipi shelters constructed of wooden poles sheathed in goat hide. Each time they approached a primitive village, in every case, the chief would hold them up before passing. With the help of their translator, they would gain permission to pass, sometimes with the help of payment.

After approximately one and a half days of travel, they made it to the foot of the mountains. In order to get to the majestic hole of water, they would have to drive through a small village where no more than a hundred people lived. The translator told the chief they wanted to pass through in search of the body of water spotted by the pilots while flying over. As were all the others, the chief was very accommodating, offering to escort them down to the place they were seeking. He led them up a stream that went right through their village and right up to the blue hole. "It was the most immaculate place you've ever seen," remembers Jim.

Making it further up the stream, they set up camp on the side of the stream that connected to the resplendent reservoir they had traveled far to reach. Jim dropped a weighted line measuring over two hundred feet in length from a point near the center of the hole. He said, "Men, there's no bottom."

Many trout were fished out of the water. In fact, there were so many that they had to build a holding well by damming up a narrow channel with big rocks to keep their dinner fresh. After an evening of fishing, they enjoyed an incredible fireside feast surrounded by unspoiled countryside and then turned in for the night.

The next morning, Jim was abruptly awoken with, "Sir, you have to come look at this." To everyone's surprise, all the fish in the holding area were turned loose, and the firewood they gathered the day before was gone.

On the opposite side of the river, they noticed a couple of men standing and watching in the distance. After an hour, the few grew in numbers to the size of a small mob. Unsettled, Jim asked the translator to come with him so they could find out if there was a problem. When they met the staring villagers, they asked if they could help them. Before the translator could finish, a rough-looking man who didn't appear to be very friendly met them. "His leg had been injured, and it looked like someone had slashed down the front of his shinbone with a machete," Jim said. The man had sunken eyes and appeared to be ill, but not to the point he couldn't express himself. So Jim asked the translator to ask the man what had happened, and they didn't want trouble. They only wanted to talk.

The translator said the man wasn't doing well, and he had been injured in a fight. He was getting weaker by the day, feeling like he was going to die. He wanted to know what they were doing near his village—the same village they had passed through the day prior.

Jim asked the injured man to follow him back across the river to their camp where he would help him. When they made camp, they brought out their medical supplies including surgical soap, sulfur, ointment, penicillin, and bandages. Next to the stream, he asked the man to put his leg in the water and then scrubbed the ulcerated skin, sloughing it off into the running stream. Cleansing the wound deeply with soap, Jim then covered the infected area with sulfur while the man propped his leg up on a boulder near them. In complete trust, the sick man watched Jim wrap his leg in gauze, something he had never saw before. Jim gave the villager several aspirin and anti-inflammatory pills with instruction on how to take them. The interpreter explained the instructions to the native and said he could leave now, that he should be better later. Very thankful, Jim's patient limped his way back down stream to the nearby village with the others.

After finishing the day by hooking more fish, one after another, they called it a night. Waking the next morning, they surprisingly discovered their fish supply had doubled, and on the other side of the stream sat a stack of firewood that would fill a boxcar. The sickly villager Jim had treated came back up to their camp minutes later with a couple of other people needing timely medical attention. He personally thanked Jim for helping him then asked if he would help the others. Jim couldn't say no, so he spent the entire day providing medical attention to the villagers while the other guys kept fishing. To Jim, only one thing would trump fishing, and that was helping less fortunate folks in need. After he went through two full footlockers of medical supplies, he couldn't do anymore. The interpreter was completely impressed by Jim's actions, and so were the villagers. From that point, they couldn't do enough for the Americans. The big guy followed Jim everywhere as a protector, not able to thank him enough, repeatedly telling him his leg was better. He was alive again.

They stayed a couple more days in peace, building a good supply of fish—much more than they could eat—and never running low of firewood.

Not wanting to leave and with permission by the village to come back anytime, they faced their next challenge. They had caught so many trout that they were going to ruin if they didn't put them on ice to chill while traveling back out 250 miles to Incirlik. On their way in, they noticed an icehouse in a small town where they would stop in transit. Two sergeants jumped out of the truck to go inside. Both smoking cigarettes at the counter, they asked for some ice. Cigarettes were hard to get in this area, particularly American smokes, so the shakedown began. The Turkish man working the counter in the ice store noticed their smokes and asked for cigarettes as payment. They tried giving him cash, but that wouldn't work for him. After several attempts, they walked out with little regard to preserve the fish they had spent days catching.

When the sergeants came back outside empty-handed, Jim ordered them to give the cigarettes up for the ice. He offered to get them more cigarettes, as the fish were not as easily replaced, so they did.

Upon returning to Incirlik AFB base with the new title of Doc Ryan, Jim was given a message from the squadron commander. Commander Everest had called from England AFB, asking that he catch the next flight out of Istanbul to New Orleans where he would be picked up in a T-33 to get him back to Alexandria so he could attend William Tell at Nellis AFB in Las Vegas (formerly the World Wide Gunnery Meet) with Gordy Williams to represent the 401st Tactical Fighter Wing.

He and Williams would match up in a shoot off to determine who would go as the primary and alternate in the competition. Williams with the 612th was a US Military Academy graduate and ultimately a second-generation major general officer. Jim and Williams were the two fighter pilots chosen from the 401st TFW from England AFB, a major honor considering the magnitude of the 401st and all the great fighter pilots that would have jumped at the chance to be a part of William Tell.

Williams, with a very bright future, was a great pilot and tough competitor, and he earned the primary position. Jim, just returning from Turkey, had only been able to practice air-to-air combat tactics and not air-to-ground due to lacking a range near Turkey to drop ordinance on. The two pilots were very close in their skill and ability, but it was Williams who was chosen first by the new commander, R.V. Travis. He'd replaced Everest, whose next command would be over the 4453rd Combat Crew Training Wing at MacDill Air Force Base, Florida. Jim was told that the primary position wouldn't do as much for his future as it would for Williams's legacy of a general and a Military Academy alumnus.

Jim would have liked the first position but was happy as an alternate. Gordy was a great friend and still is today. It helped both their careers regardless. Outside of this honor, he received more exciting news that would help shape his future. Presented with a letter from Tactical Air Command headquarters, he found out that he was chosen for a special assignment as a forward air controller with the Fourth Infantry Division of the army in Fort Lewis, Washington. The chief of the air force, General Curtis Lemay, scripted the letter, and he was to fly to Norfolk, Virginia, to Tactical Air Command headquarters, where General Walter Sweeney would honor him personally.

William Tell, in September of 1962, was a fascinating spectacle to watch, and Jim did exactly just that while he waited for a call to replace Williams if and when he had a problem and couldn't continue. Williams didn't, and he ended the three-day event with a good showing for the 401st. As soon as William Tell concluded, Jim began making arrangements for his next assignment in Fort Lewis, which he was excited about.

Flying to Virginia for the honor would make his transfer to Fort Lewis official after he went back to Alexandria to prepare for the move. It was bittersweet leaving the 401st after all the time he had spent there. He had been involved in some big assignments there, and he would come to find that he would miss another only by weeks—the Cuban missile crisis.

During a meeting between Khrushchev and Cuba's Fidel Castro that July, a secret agreement had been reached to place

Soviet nuclear missiles in Cuba; construction of several missile sites began in the late summer.

In mid-October 1962, the 401st wing was asked to respond to the Cuban missile crisis by deploying to Homestead AFB in Southern Florida, remaining on alert and ready to answer any emergency tasking caused by the blockade of Cuba—a measure put in place by a very serious John F. Kennedy.

The United States considered attacking Cuba via air and sea but decided on a military blockade instead, calling it quarantine for legal and other reasons. The United States announced that it would not permit offensive weapons to be delivered to Cuba while demanding the dismantlement and return of Soviet weapons back to the USSR. Kennedy's demands were met as an outcome.

The Cuban missile crisis led to the highest confirmed DEFCON ever—level 2. "During the Cuban Missile Crisis on October 22, 1962, the U.S. Armed Forces were ordered to DEFCON 3. On October 26, Strategic Air Command (SAC) was ordered to DEFCON 2, while the rest of the U.S. Armed Forces remained at DEFCON 3. SAC remained at DEFCON 2 until November 15".

Jim said, "Any fighter pilot who got to go down to Homestead for the Cuban Missile Crisis was the envy of the air force." He would have liked the opportunity to go with them, but he was happy about being chosen to go to Fort Lewis, where he would work closely with the Army's Fourth Infantry Division, a very big honor.

Jim had begun learning the ways of the army since 1954 while at England AFB. In between serious assignments, he had attended air-to-ground school many times, with the most recent being at Eglin AFB in Valparaiso, Florida. In between air missions, Jim honed certain specialized skills, which included public speaking, one time in front of the ROTC student body at Michigan State University, where he was commended for his presentation on the mission of the fighter pilot in the Tactical Air Command. He had also gone to airborne school earlier that year at Fort Benning, Georgia, to certify as a paratrooper through the army, which would come in handy working with an army who needed jump-qualified forward air controllers (FACs).

He could now work with any type ground unit to coordinate air strikes in simultaneous rhythm with their own firepower from the ground. This was a becoming call for some of the best up and coming fighter pilots who understood both air-to-air and air-to-ground tactics.

At this time, there was great attention on the army's intent purpose to disperse close air support (CAS) responsibilities away from the air force who was not in favor of giving up the duty to the army. The Korean War revealed important flaws in the application of CAS as it was. The big one was that USAF aircraft were not designed for CAS in the way the army needed. To them, jet fighters were too fast to adjust their targets, and strategic bombers, too big to be used on theater, making CAS much harder to implement in ground combat situations. They desired slower-moving aircraft that could get in and out of any type terrain.

During the late 1950s and early 1960s, the US Army began to identify a dedicated CAS for itself. The military began to rethink war strategy in terms of shifting from a take-ground approach, which won WWII to a more strategic forward air control method that was so instrumental in Vietnam; it was often referred to as the helicopter war. The objective was to pacify larger areas with the help of FACs flying low and slow over large blocs of territory, ferreting out the enemy and calling in airstrikes.

At the direct request of Secretary of Defense Robert McNamara, the Howze Board, a US Army group studied the question and then published a landmark report describing the need for a helicopter-based CAS requirement. Eventually adopted by the US Army was airmobility or the integration of helicopters in the role of CAS. Helicopters, not being as fast as fixed-wing aircraft and consequently more vulnerable to anti-aircraft weaponry, could utilize terrain for cover and, more importantly, had much greater battlefield persistence owing to their low speeds. The latter made them a natural complement to ground forces in the CAS role. However, this addition didn't change the air force's role in CAS, which utilized air liaison officers (ALOs) that performed mission planning and attack guidance to the army as forward air controllers (FACs). The type aircraft that a FAC utilized was much different than a fighter jet, yet required the skill of a fighter pilot.

At the time that Jim was at Fort Lewis, FACs were flying the O-1 Bird Dog, a small lightweight aircraft with a top speed of 130 miles per hour. In the O-1, they scouted the position of the enemy, marked the target from the smoke of a white phosphorous rocket or other coordinated colors to keep the enemy guessing, and then coordinated by radio the air and/or ground attack. It was a go-between position that brought army and air force efforts full circle. His time at Fort Lewis would help him build on these efforts, not to mention part of the deal he made by going to Fort Lewis included a silver lining. Once he spent time there furthering his air liaison and forward air control skills, he would be allowed to go and fly the world's fastest fighter jet, the Lockheed F-104 Starfighter—a single-engine, high-performance, supersonic interceptor aircraft that we'll get into more later. Keeping his options open while furthering his career was something Jim did by design. His options were on the opposite ends of the spectrum in terms of fast and slow aircraft and the tactics used in both.

The time came to leave for Fort Lewis after a week of packing the truck. Jim and his family took a week's leave and went through Kansas to visit both their parents since they would be well-removed from them for a while. From Kansas, it was a two-day drive into the northwest part of the United States. On the second evening, just before night fell through the mountains of Idaho, Jeanine said, "Look at that deer over there." At that moment, a second deer darted in front of their car after the diversion. When it did, they clipped the animal's hindquarters with the front of the car. Startled, Jim got out to see if there was any damage. The car was fine. The deer, on the other hand, wasn't. Still alive in the ditch, it couldn't move with a broken back, so Jim helped the deer out of its suffering with a gunshot just as a police car pulled up.

Following his moral compass, he told the officer what had happened and that he shot the deer because it was in unrecoverable pain. The policeman understood and asked Jim to follow him to do a report for the game warden's office, so they did, and the deer was processed then shared with a local orphanage. With no serious damage to the car, they continued their drive.

When reaching Fort Lewis, they checked in as usual and were assigned a very nice house near a beautiful lake next to the officers' club in lakeside base housing. The moving truck arrived, and the young family settled into their new home for the next eighteen months. Each move brought new pleasures. It was obvious things were progressing in their life, as was Jim's career.

ARMY HELICOPTERS

The Fourth Infantry utilized Grey Army Airfield in Fort Lewis to train helicopter and fixed-wing aircraft units. This was where Jim would work at the division level with the Fourth Infantry as a FAC by controlling aircraft in close support of the army. He advised battalion and subordinate company commanders and their staffs on matters pertaining to tactical air operations. His job was to promote the understanding of the USAF among army personnel by conducting briefings, lectures, demonstrations, and informal discussions on tactical air operations, which would become instrumental in the Vietnam War effort.

Fort Lewis was a big army base, with Grey Army Airfield providing a very nice runway right in the middle of the base used by all the army's aircraft, as well as USAF planes. Most were prop airlift and cargo planes, as well as the T-33 trainer jet that Jim continued to build flying time in. Larger planes were kept at McCord USAF Base just six miles away. The L-19 was the same plane the air force called the O-1 Bird Dog. "The O-1 Bird Dog was a tough little mother that would get the job done," says Jim. Working hands on with the army and flying with their pilots gave him a better idea of the way the army worked. Before a practice mission, he would meet with the army commander the evening before to go over every small detail. The next day, they would execute the mission the same way they would in a combat situation if they were at war. "I learned everything I could about the army side of the world at Fort Lewis," he said. When he wasn't performing drills and exercises, he would find other ways to practice while at the same time having a little personal fun.

Washington was wide-open country, and Jim took full advantage of the beautiful setting. He practiced his forward air control flying in the O-1 Bird Dog and, eventually, the H-13 Bell helicopter while chasing deer and prairie chickens from the air to the point they would lay down from exhaustion. Jim would stay close on their trail at low altitude, and when they hit the ground, he took off again, letting them rest to recover. There were a few times in the helicopter he would land, get out, and pick the prairie chickens up for a good coddling because they were uncatchable under normal circumstances.

Jim became close to a couple of warrant officers who were helicopter pilots that shared a common interest—bird hunting. They would fly the chopper out over fields densely populated with chucker and quail. When the birds flushed as the whirlybird approached, they watched them down, landed the chopper, then got out and flushed the birds up again on foot to shoot their limit with a shotgun. They collected the birds to clean and eat for dinner, very good eating. After several trips out, they were having so much fun that the warrant officers who were taking turns flying insisted that Jim learn to fly the helicopter too so they could get more shooting time in.

So being a fair guy, he attended another ground school to learn to fly rotary aircraft or helicopters in the H-13 chopper, which he said, "There wasn't much to it." He recalls, "Every morning, we would fly right up the beach line of Seattle to a coffee shop for practice. We flew the beach line because there were no obstacles. It was good fun."

Eventually, they started taking the UH-1 Huey out on hunting trips that would accommodate all three of them. "The Huey was better because it had more power, and it was bigger so all of us could go at the same time," he recalls with a laugh.

Hunting wasn't the only way Jim spent downtime. He became close to the deputy commander of the Fourth Infantry Division, General William Peers. It was unheard of for a senior officer to keep company with a junior officer, but this was a special circumstance since they were from different branches of the military. They also liked fishing together for salmon, golden trout, and steelhead in the Nisqually River, an on-base river they would get to by helicopter when they were not working. General Peers was another patriot who played a part in Jim's growing career.

When the United States entered World War II, Peers was recruited into the Office of Strategic Services (OSS). He joined Detachment 101, which carried out guerrilla operations against the Japanese in the China India Burma Theater. As commander of all OSS operations in China south of the Yangtze River, he led a Nationalist Chinese parachute-commando unit into Nanking, securing the former Chinese capital from the Japanese and Communist Chinese before the armistice.

Peers joined the CIA after World War II, establishing the agency's first training program. During the Korean War, he directed covert operations by Chinese Nationalist troops into the southern part of the People's Republic of China from secret bases in Burma.

Upon his return from China, he attended the prestigious Army War College and afterward held a series of intelligence and staff positions. With his Asian insurgency warfare expertise, it was inevitable that his career would prosper during the Vietnam War. At its beginning, Peers was the assistant deputy chief of staff for special operations. The next year, he became special assistant for counterinsurgency and special activities for the joint chiefs of staff.

In January 1967, as a major general, he was named the thirty-second commanding officer of the Fourth Infantry Division. After fourteen months, he was promoted to lieutenant general and commanded the fifty thousand American soldiers of the corps-level I Field Force, Vietnam. Based in the Central Highlands, The I Field Force comprised some of the most aggressive American Divisions in Vietnam, including the 1st Cavalry Division, 101st Airborne Division, and the 173rd Airborne Brigade. Peers also coordinated the operations of four South Vietnamese and the two elite South Korean divisions sent as that country's contribution. Under his leadership, allied troops decisively defeated Viet Cong guerrillas and NVA regulars in the battles of Dak To in November 1967 and Duc Lap in August 1968.

In 1969, Peers was ordered by General William Westmoreland to investigate the My Lai Massacre, being selected because of his reputation for fairness and objectivity. The My Lai Massacre, the most shocking episode of the Vietnam War, was a mass murder of between 347 and 504 unarmed civilians in South Vietnam on March 16, 1968. It was committed by the US Army soldiers from the Company C of the First Battalion, Twentieth Infantry Regiment, Eleventh Brigade of the Twenty-Third (Americal) Infantry Division. Victims included women, men, children, and infants. Some of the women were gang raped and their bodies mutilated.

In 1970, Peers issued a very thorough and critical report on the incident called the *Peers Commission*. Hugh Thompson, along with his helicopter crew, were the only soldiers who attempted to stop the massacre. He said this of Peers's report:

> The Army had Peers conduct the investigation. He conducted a very thorough investigation. Congress did not like his investigation at all because he pulled no punches, and he recommended court-martial for I think 34 people, not necessarily for the murder but for the cover-up.

"General Peers was a great friend of mine, and we fished all the time together while at Fort Lewis. We remained friends long after that too," said Jim.

It was new for the army to work with an ALO and FAC at the time, but it was a match made in heaven. Showcasing what two armed forces could accomplish while working together was displayed in a big way through fire power demonstrations in front of the military's highest command, their wives, dignitaries, and public officials. There was a great deal of preparation leading up to the shows, and it was the ultimate opportunity to be noticed.

With grandstand seating in front of a vast firing range, the army and air force showcased their skills through sequence firing on a target by air and ground artillery with minimum time intervals between artillery fire and air-delivered ordnance. With the highest air force and army generals present, Jim would fly the Fourth Infantry's four-star general C.E. Hutchin Jr. to a landing platform before the grandstand in an Army UH-1 Huey for a grandiose entrance. Once landing on the platform in front of the crowd, the general would introduce Jim as his own air force pilot and explain to the audience what to expect. From there, Jim would go and play his part in the demonstration as a FAC on the ground or display his piloting skills in a helicopter or jet.

On 5 May 1963, the first strike command exercise called Coulee Crest occurred. Lasting fifteen days, the display featured battles for air superiority and line-fire maneuvers between two army divisions and Air Force Strike Command in Yakima, Washington. It was held at the bottom of a thousand-foot canyon in Yakima and gained widespread attention.

With a radio in hand close to General Peers at the top of the canyon, Jim orchestrated simultaneous fire from the air and ground on the same target, calculated to the second. It was a spectacle for many who had never witnessed such a display. For others who had seen these type demonstrations before, it was above the rest. It was said in a letter by Major Russell Christensen of the 4501st Support Squadron and ALO for the Fourth Infantry Division, "During the joint Air Force-Army exercise "Coulee Crest" Captain Ryan did the most outstanding job of forward air controlling I have ever seen." This statement was concurred by W.D. Dunham, brigadier general and director of operations of the Twelfth Air Force.

Jim had gotten really good at bringing the army and air force together to work in unison. He said, "When you see an artillery shell hit the ground at the same time the jets rolled out after dropping their ordnance, you know you are doing well." As he suspected, he did do well, and it was noticed by the army who showed their appreciation. Below is a transcribed letter from Major General Hutchin Jr. to Twelfth Air Force Command.

11 April 1964

To: Commander of 4501st Support Squadron, Waco, TX

During the period 10 November 1963 to 11 April 1964, Captain James C. Ryan has served as a Forward Air Controller with the 4th Infantry Division.

On several occasions I have personally observed Captain Ryan's spirited and conscientious performance of duty. This attitude coupled with his outstanding knowledge of Air Force capabilities and their adaptability to the support of ground forces has been a deciding factor in the highly successful participation of this organization in joint exercises.

Captain Ryan's congeniality, initiative, enthusiasm and high degree of professional competence has served as the basis for a most rewarding relationship with my staff. His relationship has instilled within my staff and units a greater degree of appreciation for the support available within the Tactical Air Command. It has enhanced the training program of the 4th Infantry Division in that it has been instrumental in broadening the scope of our objectives.

During the period cited Captain Ryan's performance of duty has garnered high praise and reflected great credit upon himself and the United States Air Force.

C.E. Hutchin, Jr.
Major General, USA
Commanding

Even though Jim's main focus at Fort Lewis was forward air control and flying the 0-1 Bird Dog and UH-1 Huey, he also wanted to keep his jet skills up. While doing just that, he remembers a historical moment, a sad day. Often, he would fly a T-33 into the air base in Fort Lewis from McChord Field, only six miles away. On 22 November 1963, Jim remembers entering the flight pattern to land at Grey Army Airfield when he heard the announcement over the radio that President John F. Kennedy had been assassinated in Dallas, Texas. It was a sad day near the end of his time in Washington and one that he remembers. "I'm not a democrat, but I always liked John Kennedy," said Jim. "He had guts."

June of 1964 came, and Jim's time at Fort Lewis had been fulfilled. It was invaluable experience to work with the army, and he had impressed, leaving a good taste in their mouth about the air force. It was time for him to take his next assignment. It would land him in the fastest fighter jet on the planet, working closely with the world's first fighter jet pilot to shoot down a fighter jet, as well as the lead pilot who flew the toughest stunts in the movie *Air Cadet,* which originally inspired him. Their job would be to train the German Luftwaffe pilots to fly the F-104. Jim would leave the cockpit of the O-1 Bird Dog with a top speed of 130 mph to fly at speeds in excess of two thousand miles per hour.

JABARA

Leaving the cold of Fort Lewis, Jim and his family made way for a much warmer Phoenix, Arizona, where they would call Luke AFB home. The dry heat of Arizona provided ideal flying conditions year-round, the perfect setting to train the German Luftwaffe (air force) in the second stage of a two-stage program under Air Training Command. The first stage of training the West Germans was basic training in the T-37 and T-38 jet aircraft at Williams AFB in Arizona. Second stage was advanced training in the F-104G, the fastest fighter jet in the world at the time. By mid-July 1964, (thirty-five) F-104s were assigned to Luke AFB to be used in the process. On 26 August 1964, there were (fourteen) USAF F-104 instructor pilots who graduated in only the second class conducted at Luke, Jim being one of them. He would work with the 4512th Combat Crew Training Squadron (CCTS) supervising and instructing Luftwaffe student pilots in advanced fighter employment techniques in the F-104G aircraft. Instructor responsibilities included briefing, execution, and critique of combat crew training flights including transition, formation, aerobatics, air-to-ground gunnery, bombing, rocketry, air-to-air gunnery, air-to-air radar, radar navigation, and radar bombing.

The state-of-art Lockheed F-104 Starfighter caught the attention of the world as a single-engine, high-performance, supersonic interceptor aircraft originally developed for the United States Air Force, and it was operated by the air forces of more than a dozen nations from 1958 to 2004.

The F-104 featured a radical wing design. Most jet fighters of the period used a swept-wing or delta-wing planform. This allowed a reasonable balance between aerodynamic performance, lift, and internal space for fuel and equipment. Lockheed's tests, however, determined that the most efficient shape for high-speed, supersonic flight was a very small, straight, mid-mounted, trapezoidal wing.

The F-104 Starfighter was designed to use the General Electric J79 turbojet engine, fed by side-mounted intakes with fixed inlet cones optimized for supersonic speeds. Unlike some supersonic aircraft, the F-104 did not have variable-geometry inlets. Its thrust-to-drag ratio was excellent, allowing a maximum speed well in excess of Mach 2: the top speed of the Starfighter was limited more by the aluminum airframe structure and the temperature limits of the engine compressor than by thrust or drag (which gave an aerodynamic maximum speed of Mach 2.2) .

It was equipped with state-of-the-art avionics including ranging radar, a tactical air navigation system, and an AN/ARC-34 UHF Radio. One of the drawbacks of the jet was the basic armament—the 20 mm (.79 in) M61 Vulcan Gatling gun. This weapon frequently had shell ejection problems resulting in avionic problems and crashes. The Starfighter was the first aircraft to carry the new weapon, which had a rate of fire of six thousand rounds per minute. The cannon was mounted in the lower part of the port fuselage fed from a 725-round drum behind the pilot's seat.

There wasn't much room for ordnance under the wings, choices being two AIM-9 Sidewinder air-to-air missiles on the pylons or external fuel tanks. Despite the faults of the F-104, it was an incredibly fast aircraft that Jim says was super fun to fly.

When he arrived, he met face-to-face with his new commander of the 4540th Combat Crew Training Group (CCTG). He recognized the face from an earlier time back in Wichita, Kansas, at a parade with his wife, Jeanie, who was a high school girlfriend at the time. They witnessed a war hero riding the nose of an F-80 Shooting Star aircraft rolling down the street, leading a parade. It was Wichita native James "Jabby" Jabara, who had returned from Korea on stateside leave for a publicity tour. Jim said, "I remember seeing Jabara for the first time in the parade at the end of high school. He was a hero. When I found myself getting to work side by side with him, it was an amazing thing."

Jim remembers what an incredible pilot Jabara was, another patriot he was taken under the wing of. Let's take a closer look at Jabby.

Jabara rose to the top of the fighter business like a lightning bolt. It started with over 100 European missions flown in a P-51 before age twenty. Within his first weeks in Korea, he killed four MiGs, only one short of the total necessary to become an ace. His squadron that was due to rotate back to the States would take him with it, so in order to avoid leaving the war, he transferred to another squadron. He got number five and six less than a month later with the new squadron, making him the world's first jet ace.

It's been said that James sang the loudest in the club, made more noise than the others, dressed on the extreme side for the military—those sorts of things. But however disturbing he might have been at times to military regimen on the ground, his cocky aggressiveness and predictable courage were unquestioned assets in the air war. Therefore, when the Wichita pilot had two kills, Lt. Col. John Meyer singled him out in response to Major General Earle Partridge's request to choose someone with the characteristics to become a jet ace. "I decided on Jabara as the most likely candidate. Anything that was a milk run, he didn't go, and anything up on the Yalu, he did go, and we saw that he was in the flight-leader position, which was usually the best."

The mission of May 20, 1951, was no milk run. About 5:00 p.m., two flights of Sabres, twenty-eight planes, engaged fifty MiGs near Sinuiju in northwest Korea. Because the Sabres dropped their wing tanks when entering battle to achieve better aerodynamics, fuel limitations meant battles seldom lasted over ten minutes. Jabara's time was busy.

His initial problem was that one of his wing tanks failed to release, requiring him to fly with both hands on the stick. The air force rule was that in such a situation, a pilot was to disengage and return to base. Jabara instead attacked a group of three MiGs and got on the tail of one of them. No evasive maneuver would shake the American pilot, and the MiG eventually took three machine-gun bursts in the fuselage and wing. The enemy plane did two violent snap rolls, began to smoke, and then belched flames before falling into an uncontrolled spin. Jabara and his wingman saw the pilot bail out and went into a tight 360-degree turn to follow the plane all the way down to confirm its destruction. "All I could see of him was a whirl of fire," said Jabara. "I had to break off because there was another MiG on my tail." With no time to think about becoming America's first jet ace, Jabara accelerated his airplane back into the battle above him. But as he reached 20,000 feet, he noticed a difficulty perhaps more serious than the drag of his wing tank. His companion had gotten diverted by enemy fire and was no longer with him. Fighting in pairs was essential in jet fighter battles, as the speed and G-forces in aerial maneuvering were so great that the attacker had to concentrate fully on the target and rely on the wingman to cover him and warn of other planes approaching. The rule was that if you were separated from your wingman, you disengaged and returned to base. Jabara instead attacked another group of MiGs.

The engagement seemed successful; a MiG, hit in the wings and tail section, flamed out and spiraled to the left. Jabara cut back power and then opened his speed brakes to follow the airplane down to 6,500 feet, making sure it hit the ground. But things were not as smooth as they seemed. "I was following this MiG down," Jabara said later, "when all of a sudden, I heard a noise that sounded like a popcorn machine right in my cockpit. I looked back and saw two MiGs firing at me, and I could see black puffs from their cannons exploding all around me. I broke down to the left, closed my speed brakes, and opened my power. For about two minutes, we went round and round, they shooting at me while I tried my best to get away. I didn't dare break out because I would have been too good a target."

At the point of ultimate discouragement, Jabara heard two of his friends, Morris Pitts and Gene Holley, talking on their radios about a lone F-86 under attack. Although his voice was strained due to the G-forces of his tight turn, Jabby Jabara was able to identify himself and to say that he knew too dammed well that there was a lone F-86 being shot at. As a courtesy, Pitts said, "Call me if you need some help." Jabara, low on fuel and hotly pursued, allowed that he could use some. On seeing the two approaching Sabres, the MiG wingman fled, but the one pursuing Jabara, intent on his sights, remained. The four planes flew for some time, Holley firing at the MiG, Pitts protecting Holley, the MiG firing at Jabara, and Jabara trying to avoid fire from two sources. Finally the MiG broke off, and the Sabre group, low on fuel, turned south toward home, landing just at dusk.

There was a party that evening at Kimpo. Jabara drank his usual large quantity of beer with the usual minimal obvious effects, smoked a number of cigars, and used his hands in characteristic fashion to show the battle while he talked about it. He did not neglect in the excitement to warn the other pilots against becoming sitting ducks as he had by trying to attack without a wingman, but it was clear that at least for that day he himself had felt invincible.

It was a special day for James Jabara, to be sure, the day he became America's first jet ace. He was hailed at the time and since as the world's first jet ace. Technically, account must be taken of German aces piloting the Messerschmitt 262 jet at the end of World War II, but it should be remembered that the planes they shot down were not also jets.

Whatever titles are appropriate, however, what is remarkable is that for Jabara, May 20, 1951 wasn't a terribly unusual day. It was his sixty-third Korean mission of an eventual 163. He was to have two other days when he was to down two planes and would become, in that war, a triple ace. He won a Distinguished Service Cross, the nation's second highest decoration, on May 20, 1951, but he was to add a silver star and oak leaf cluster to that for repeat performances. He earned a stateside leave for a publicity tour which he did not want and media attention that had not been the object of his quest. He wanted to return to his canopied cockpit and carry on his business as soon as his back muscles recovered from the strain of in-flight maneuvers. "I can hardly sit down," he told reporters who met him in Japan on his way home to Wichita, "my fanny is so sore." They gave him a press biography form then containing the question, "Anything that might be of news interest?" Jabara wrote, "None."

If working with James Jabara at Luke AFB wasn't memorable enough for Jim, there was someone else who put his time there over the top, another notorious fighter pilot who had something to do with him joining the air force. It was Leon Gray who, as commander of Williams AFB in 1950 and '51, had a cameo role in the movie *Air Cadet*, the film that inspired Jim to become a fighter pilot back in Kansas. Beside Gray's brief part in the movie, he did all the lead flying for the film in the T-33. Another patriot who indirectly inspired Jim would now directly impact him as one of the air forces most experienced with the new F-104G.

Here's more on Leon Gray. During WWII, Gray commanded a reconnaissance group that flew the P-38 Lightning over occupied Europe to take photos of enemy positions. While doing his dangerous job, he was once shot down by a German fighter pilot, which earned him the Distinguished Service Cross as well as awards from England and France. He became the first jet pilot in 1946 to win the Bendix Trophy, an annual award given for the fastest trip from the West Coast to the Eastern United States. He won the trophy again in 1947, flying from California to Cleveland in four hours, four minutes. While at Williams AFB, he established the Acrojets Flying Team—the first officially recognized USAF precursor to the Thunderbird Team, which succeeded in 1953. In 1958, he became commander of the 4700th Air Defense Wing, Geiger Field, Washington, which was the first Mach 2 flying command in the world, home of the F-104. In 1959, he was the winner of the William Tell worldwide weapons meet (rocket and missile firing), flying the F-104 Starfighter jet.

This was a milestone era in the fighter business, truly a dynamic time in aviation. It was the height of jet aviation design and military diversity, unlike anything we've seen since. It seemed that every new assignment Jim took, the best and most influential fighter pilots in the world, who left an unprecedented mark on the history of the industry, surrounded him.

Another instructor at Luke that was a part of this special time in history was Berlin B. Huffman "BB" who had flown combat missions in Europe and Korea. He and Jim would take very similar career paths and become lifelong friends. "I met BB at Luke AFB, and he looked the part, like the kind of guy you wanted to be around. Boy, was I right, he was one of the best pilots I ever had the pleasure of flying with," says Jim.

They, along with twelve other instructors, trained the German pilots in the F-104. "Jim said that the F-104 was intimidating to the Germans. They hadn't been in anything that fast, and it scared them."

This was a matter of fact recorded in history. The first German Starfighters were the Lockheed-built two-seat F-104Fs, which were initially used in the USA to train German instructors. At that time, the F-104Fs were painted with standard USAF insignia and carried USAF serial numbers. These machines were then handed over, and they were repainted in Luftwaffe insignia, and assigned German serial numbers. From there the Luftwaffe became the primary user of the Starfighter, operating over thirty-five percent of all F-104s built. Luftwaffe F-104Gs came from all five production lines of the Starfighter consortium. The West German Luftwaffe received a total of 915 Starfighters and, during its period of service with the German armed forces, lost 270 German Starfighters in accidents, just fewer than thirty percent of the total force. About 110 pilots were killed.

Jim was good at his job as an instructor and commended by his superiors, but he found himself needing something more, which he soon would discover.

Officer Effectiveness Report

12 April – 4 March 65

This officer performed additional duty in the Group Operations Division as a scheduling officer. He performed this duty in a highly commendable manner. I have observed his performance as an F-104G Instructor Pilot and there is no doubt about his exceptionally fine ability. Promote him to temporary major in advance of his contemporaries.

James Jabara
Colonel, USAF 4540th CCTG Commander

In late 1965, Jim had an opportunity to attend ground school in Florida to keep his forward air control skills up, something he enjoyed and missed. This trip would be an eye-opener that led him away from the F-104, which he also loved flying, straight into war as a forward air control officer and FAC. After readjusting to the speed difference between the F-104 and 01-Bird Dog, Jim clearly recognized his calling as an air liaison officer for the army. Even though flying jets was a thrill, to him, the real need was in forward air control. This became more and more obvious all the time.

Upon completing the training, he ran into another fighter pilot who he recognized from Aviation Cadet Training. He was in full uniform and decorated from head to toe in medals. Jim asked, "Where in the world did you get all that?" The young fighter pilot answered he'd just done a tour in Vietnam as a forward air controller, filling Jim in on the need for close air support in the jungles of South East Asia, and said that Jim could do the same thing.

That's all it took for him to realize what he wanted to do. He returned to Luke AFB and told Jabara that he was going to volunteer for the war as a FAC. Jabara answered to him that he didn't blame him and was soon going to go himself with an F-4 Phantom squadron. It was 1965, and Jim would soon see combat for the first time.

GOING TO VIETNAM

Jim attended jungle survival school in the Philippines en route to the war. Survival school was one full week of lecture at the base followed by a week in the most primitive jungle setting he had ever experienced, similar to what he would see in South Vietnam. They learned to find food and water and build shelter out of bamboo and palm leaves in preparation for surviving alone. Next, all the trainees were trucked about twenty-five miles deep into the jungle and then turned loose on foot. Their task was to evade capture and make it back to camp. Asian natives called Negritos populated the same area and were instructed to apprehend all the trainees to be awarded a hundred-pound bag of rice for each American caught. When captured, they were escorted back to camp, stripped, and then put into a bamboo jail hardly tall enough for a dog. Apprehended, that's where they would spend their last night before leaving for war.

The short of it was they were all captured and escorted back the long way by the adept natives. Jim and his partner would go into jail around midnight of the second day from being turned loose.

"We were partnered up in groups of two to give us more of an advantage. I came up with a great plan to evade capture and become the first group to successfully make it back to camp without being grabbed. The plan? We would trek in the opposite direction for a half day then cross over two ridgelines and then leisurely walk down the draw until there. Once crossing over to walk into camp, singing and having a good time, we would call it a successful quest. That's not the way it went," recalls Jim.

In reality, Jim and his partner Peewee walked a couple hours from where they were left to find a hillside full of wild sweet potatoes; it was a good thing because they were starved. Sweet potatoes were the best and easiest type food to find in the jungle. "With my long-bladed knife, I dropped down to my knees to dig up the potatoes. When I had all my flying suit pockets full, I told Peewee I could see and hear a stream just down in the draw below. I would head down to cool off from the heat, rest, and wash off the potatoes. Peewee, with fewer potatoes, decided to stay on the hill and gather more food. He would join me after a while. So I went without him," recalls Jim.

The stream was as pretty as what he grew up around Lodi, Oklahoma, as a child. He lay in the water, resting and cleaning potatoes for about an hour. Then he heard Peewee calling his name loudly, saying, "Jim, we're caught! Where are you?" He kept repeating this over and over again. Jim immediately dropped over the bank of the deepest part of the water to pull vines and vegetation over him to hide. He cut a hollow reed for underwater breathing and then submerged. It wasn't long before Peewee and his new friends made it down to the stream, where they started uncovering the lined edges. All the time, Peewee continued to holler out, "Jim, where are you? We're caught!" Eventually, they uncovered Jim, and he was stuck like his partner. As the natives grabbed him, he said, "Yes, Peewee, we're caught thanks to you."

It was probably for the best though, because Peewee wasn't much of an outdoorsman, and more than likely, he wouldn't have been able to keep up with Jim, who was serious about making it back without getting caught. Peewee could have been hurt trying. What's worse was that he was on his way to the Vietnam War soon, and he was not quite ready.

The Negritos kept their capture streak alive, with everyone in the survival class behind bamboo bars. "Peewee and I were the last to arrive at midnight under a full moon. I remember being so hungry I could have eaten anything, but nothing would be available until 9:00 a.m. that morning," said Jim.

There was a short pudgy native on guard, slumped up against the cage the trainees were in. "I made it over quietly to where he was near asleep, then in my best sign language, asked him if he had anything to eat. I was hungry." The guard indicated to Jim that he didn't have anything but went into the jungle with his rifle in hand to later return with a large black bird, like a crow. The Negrito made a small fire and placed a black pot full of stream water over the burning embers. Then he put the plucked bird inside whole, guts and all.

Over the next hour, he cooked the bird and made a bamboo bowl by cutting a big piece off at the joint. Then he served Jim some bird stew. "To my surprise, it wasn't bad, considering how hungry I was. We became friends," he said. Later that morning, several helicopters arrived and took the group of readied men back to Clark Air Force Base in the Philippines where they began. From there, they would go to Saigon and then to war. Before Jim boarded the chopper, the Negrito who made him a late night meal hugged him. Jim states this particular survival training, which wasn't his first one, was the best he ever experienced, and it was good preparation for the next year in II Corp Vietnam.

On 1 March 1966, they boarded a Flying Tiger Airlines C-121 Constellation to Tan Son Nhut AB, Vietnam, for permanent duty. The United States unleashed a tremendous amount of air power during the Vietnam War. It would be controlled by the most widespread forward air control effort in history. As the headquarters for the South Vietnamese Air Force, Tan Son Nhut was primarily a command base, with most operational units using nearby Bien Hoa AB. Tactical Air Control System (TACS) was in close proximity to the headquarters of the VNAF and USAF forces in South Vietnam, and commanders of both air forces utilized its facilities. Subordinate to TACS was the Direct Air Support Centers (DASC) assigned to each of corps' areas (I DASC–Da Nang AB, DASC Alpha-Nha Trang AB, II DASC-Pleiku AB, III DASC-Bien Hoa AB, and IV DASC-Cần Thơ AB). DASCs were responsible for the deployment of aircraft located within their sector in support of ground operations. Operating under each DASC were numerous Tactical Air Control Party (TACPs), manned by one or more Vietnamese Air Force (VNAF) and USAF personnel posted with the South Vietnamese Army (ARVN) ground forces. A communications network linked these three levels of command and control, giving the TACS overall control of the South Vietnamese air situation at all times.

The C-121 landed and then taxied over to a small terminal building in a remote part of the air base at the north end of the ramp. Jim, along with the others, was instructed to walk directly inside without stopping to talk or letting anyone in between them, as it could be dangerous. The enemy was elusive because they all dressed the same in black cotton shirts and trousers, similar to pajamas. "Even though not all of them were sided with the North Vietnamese Army, we had to treat them as such because you couldn't tell who was and who wasn't until they took a shot at you," said Jim. He checked in with the Central Base Processing Office (CBPO) inside to find a very loose reporting protocol ran primarily by female military personnel along with some local civilians. In fact, he found himself telling them what to do in the end. Late in the evening, when he gave them his identification, he was told to come back in the morning because they were shut down until then. He asked, "Where do I stay tonight?"

The woman told him, while pointing toward a number of buildings, "Walk that way to find a bed and then come back in the morning."

He found a bed, didn't sleep much, and early the next morning, he went back to check in before the airport started to bustle. At this time, Tan Son Nhut Airport was reported as the busiest airport in the world, with a mix of air traffic that approached chaotic proportions.

Meeting him at the desk was the woman from the night before. "Where do you want to go?" she asked. Not having a specific assignment other than to report to CBPO at this air base, he was a little taken back to find out he had a choice of where he went to do combat. He wasn't familiar with the army divisions stationed in Vietnam, where they were geographically assigned, or anything else pertaining to where he was supposed to go. Not completely sure of the situation, he mentioned he was there for forward air control. Familiar with the term, they told him he was in the right place. He then asked, "Can you tell me where Major Bob Ruby is?" They told him that Ruby was in An Khe as the ALO with the First Air Cavalry Division-Tactical Air Control party. Ready to get the show on the road, Jim said, "That's where I want to go then. I'll go where he is." They told Jim he would need to go to Pleiku, the first-step headquarters in An Khe, and contact Major Ruby from there.

Just when he didn't think matters could get more confusing, he asked, "Okay, how do I get there?"

They said, "That's up to you. You'll have to go out on the ramp and find a ride."

Who would have guessed reporting for war would have been so liberating, but after all, that's why we fight—to ensure that we have freedom to make our own choices. Even when showing up for combat, an American has choices.

When Jim walked outside, he noticed a multitude of C-130 cargo aircraft flying in and out in constant numbers. Planes were landing on the runway to fall in line for pallets of cargo. Never shutting down their engines, they would pull up to load then fly back out to deliver to the war zone and then return for another load. He walked up to a C-130 crew that was loading pallets on their aircraft and asked, "I need to get to Pleiku. Can you guys get me there?" They said they were going there shortly, and he was welcome to jump onboard. They would have to stop in Nha Trang first. With few questions asked, Jim boarded and made it to Pleiku.

When getting there, he thanked the pilots for the ride, grabbed his bag, then proceeded to the ops building. Jim contacted Major Ruby at headquarters in An Khe, who was happy to hear from him, since they hadn't spoken but a few times since Jim was with the 614th TFS at England AFB under his command. He didn't waste any time inviting him to An Khe to work with the 1st Air Cavalry, 1st Brigade who needed a good ALO and FAC. The 1st Air Cavalry Division (Airmobile) is one of the most decorated combat divisions of the United States Army, and its 1st Brigade is a renowned combat aviation helicopter outfit set up with a combination of attack helicopters. At the time, the 1st Air Cavalry had approximately six hundred helicopters in Vietnam, and during their service in Vietnam, they would incur more casualties than any other division of the military (5,444 killed in action).

He would be their 1st Brigade ALO and perform forward air control for them exclusively under the command of Major Ruby, the Division ALO for the 1st Air Cavalry and chief of the Air Force Tactical Control Party at An Khe.

Arriving in An Khe at Division headquarters, Jim met with Major Ruby who gave him the details on the 1st Brigade. From his letterbox window surrounded by sandbags stacked three layers deep, he pointed up to the top of a hill where they were located. Near the end of the conversation, all hell broke loose. The headquarters was under a mortar attack, the ground trembling. Major Ruby took Jim out to show him what to do in a situation like this. They ran to jump into a long foxhole for safety. People were rolling over the sides of the hole and landing on others already hunkered down at the bottom.

After the attack ended, Ruby took Jim to the chow hall for a bite to eat and then out to a large tent with cots for sleeping. He then said he would come back for him in the morning to see that he made it to his new brigade commander.

The next morning, they took a jeep down a highway east from An Khe toward Qui Nhon, where he would board a helicopter to fly to the camp where the First Brigade (Iron Horse Brigade) was for the time. They moved around a lot.

Shortly after settling in, he met Col. Archie Hyle, Commander of the First Brigade who told Jim he wanted him close at all times. When not flying as a FAC, he would be with Colonel Hyle in his Command and Control UH-1D helicopter for purposes of CAS. Hyle had true grit and feared very little; him and Jim would get along great. They became close in a short time, Jim becoming his personal helicopter pilot. Over and over again, Jim asked him to fly the helicopter and eventually wore Hyle down to the point he agreed to let him try, just to shut Jim up. To Hyle's surprise,

Jim was a great helicopter pilot trained by the Fourth Infantry in Fort Lewis, Washington. From that point forward, Jim flew the command chopper for him, and did it often. If he wasn't flying forward air control in the 0-1 Bird Dog, he was flying Archie in the UH-1D. He was always flying something, and woke up daily to take flight for a fight, be it plane or chopper.

On 24 May 1966, Jim was flying a FAC mission only thirty miles north of Pleiku in Dak To where a Civilian Irregular Defense Group (CIDG) Green Beret camp was. The CIDG camps were established along the borders of South Vietnam in order to both maintain surveillance of enemy infiltration and to provide support and training to isolated Montagnard villagers, who bore the brunt of the fighting in the isolated areas.

Jim's first flight in Vietnam the day before was flying over the same isolated area with an instructor in the back of the aircraft to familiarize him, like a checkout ride. This was his second flight there with the First Brigade, one that wouldn't be as standard. Going back out by himself this time, he got a call that an O-1 pilot was down due west of Pleiku. He responded with confirmation he would check it out. Over a wide clear field surrounded by thick groves of banana trees, it didn't take him long to spot the plane that was nosed into a grove at the edge. Jim circled a few times, the entire time calling without ever making contact with the downed pilot. He decided to get closer. Flying low and slow hugging the ground, he noticed a trail from the opening into the jungle. Suddenly, he was being shot at, a new experience.

He banked away as fast as the O-1 would go and circled back around to notice a large group of VC coming out of the jungle up the hill to the area where the downed pilot was. Pitching out at one hundred feet or so to make an exit from the heavy gunfire, he traveled a mile from the site in direction back to safety. Then he had a revelation. "I can't leave now. What am I doing?" he asked himself. He turned back around, scared like crazy, deciding to weigh his odds against the enemy. He could see and hear the tracer bullets flying by his plane while making passes so low that his landing gear almost touched ground.

When things got really hot, he again found himself trying to leave. Then, as before, he decided not to flee; he had to help this man. It was a subconscious discernment. Before making the turn, he thought to himself, *Lord, this is a test, and I must do what I can to help.* In the plane, alone—or perhaps not—he said, *Please let my wife and children know that I love them, and I have to help this pilot who doesn't stand a chance without me. It's my job, regardless of the outcome.*

Then without hesitation, he sucked the 0-1 around as sharp as he could, going in hard toward the enemy. Firing the few smoke rockets he was carrying, he let the VC know that he wasn't leaving without a fight. They ducked to the ground, having trouble shooting up from their bellies, and Jim kept coming back, lower with each pass.

He called Tactical Air Control to send help, and they responded with encouragement. They answered that they had four F-100s on the way, along with four F-4 Phantoms, and to hold on. "Keep the enemy in sight," they said.

Out of rockets, he kept low to the ground, diving at the enemy to slow their pursuit for the downed aircraft. Using everything he could, Jim dipped his wing tips to try and knock the VC to the ground. The next pass, he nosed down lower, trying to drive the spinning propeller into their chests if given the slightest chance. The entire time, he flew through heavy gunfire, dishing it back any way he could. With his windows locked open, he drew the pistol from his hip and fired out the windows until he ran out of bullets.

He radioed to army ground operations, who told him there were five Green Beret about five miles away making good time. While keeping communications going with air and ground forces, he kept his eye on the VC trying to retreat into the jungle from the open field.

Jim heard the roar of the jets coming from the distance. The fighter jets had arrived, and he was ready to coordinate the strike. The Green Berets were now two miles away, so Jim instructed them to take cover and stay back until further notice. The F-100s dumped first. Then the F-4s lit the place up without getting too close to the downed plane. With the jungle on fire, flames licked thirteen enemies dead, and the rest fled for safety. When the air strike was over, Jim flew in low and slow to see as much as possible to do a bomb damage assessment (BDA). The report reflected total annihilation surrounding the untouched O-1 that remained nose in, no report from the pilot still. When the Green Berets arrived, they reported the O-1 pilot was dead on impact from a bullet that had gone through his cockpit, hitting a day-night flare on his survival vest, igniting and burning him badly from the chest up. "After all of that, the pilot was already dead. It was my first combat mission, and I was never scared again," said Jim.

Later, he made it back to Pleiku, where he was notified he would be put in for the Distinguished Flying Cross medal for heroic flying, something he did receive for his actions the second day in Vietnam.

Citation To Accompany the Award of
The Distinguished Flying Cross

To James C. Ryan

Captain James C. Ryan distinguished himself by heroism while participating in aerial flight as a Forward Air
Controller in Pleiku Province, Republic of Vietnam on 24
May 1966. On that date, Captain Ryan came to the aid
of friendly ground forces attempting to rescue a downed
Air Force pilot. Remaining in the area for over two hours
below five hundred feet, he braved intense hostile ground
fire while directing close support sorties and conducting
innumerable harassment passes at the opposing forces
until the friendly wounded forces could be evacuated. The
outstanding heroism and selfless devotion to duty displayed by Captain Ryan reflect great credit upon himself
and the United States Air Force.

FAC IN SEA

Jim and the first brigade did a great deal of reconnaissance work to seek out the enemy. They roamed widespread areas throughout II Corp and, often, villages occupied by Montagnard, who are indigenous people occupying the Central Highlands of Vietnam. The term *Montagnard* means mountain people in French and is a carryover from the French colonial period. They were the people caught in the middle during the war due to the fact they were constantly confronted by the VC to take up arms against the United States or be killed. "They were often given a weapon and enough bullets to get them killed, maybe two or three at most," said Jim. The United States would try and get to them to provide protection before they were faced by the VC, and at first contact, American soldiers never knew where they stood with them—friend or foe?

During the push, the First Cavalry confiscated mass quantities of guns by chance of stumbling up on them or, more likely, by getting a tip, sometimes from the Montagnard. The First Brigade built a huge stockpile of enemy guns that were sometimes traded to other army divisions and brigades for something else.

"I was sleeping and stashing my clothing and gear wherever I could find a place, which changed on a daily basis," recalls Jim. He was tired of calling a raggedy tent as home. After the big push through II Corp, he made arrangements with Colonel Hyle to trade weapons for materials to build a house. Hyle agreed by designating an area right by his own house for Jim and the five other FACs that were assigned to the Tactical Air Control Party of the First Cavalry Division. Major Ruby liked the idea, agreeing it was good for his men to have a place of their own, so Jim got right on it. Once the FACs leveled the ground for their new project, they traded for lumber, nails, hammers, saws, and everything needed for construction. None of them had done any type building work before, but war had a way of making people resourceful and ambitious. When they were not flying the O-1 Bird Dog, something they kept in the air around the clock, they were working on the construction of the house. As an ALO and FAC, Jim split time between the O-1 and the commander's UH-1 with Colonel Hyle in addition to leading the construction of the house they called the House built by the FACs; they made a sign which was proudly displayed on the front door. It was the finest home on the base, something he's very proud of today. He made trips to Saigon to buy furnishings including big leather recliners, a refrigerator, and slot machines for entertainment. Jim said, "We planted banana trees in the backyard close to the grill, and we had the only attached shower on base. I also picked Archie up a leather chair in Saigon always including him in everything I got."

Jim became an expert at much more than building houses in Vietnam. His FAC skills soared, you could say, with 377 combat missions in the O-1 plus 214 hours in the Huey. One example of such a mission followed the morning after they completed the house.

The sun glimmered through the glass of the 0-1 Bird Dog as he flew alone over Northeast II Corp. "I had no direct orders for the day but to fly a visual reconnaissance mission or in simple terms, troll for fire from the enemy. I was looking for a fight," said Jim. He flew the slow-moving aircraft at less than five hundred feet from the ground so he could see well. With no firepower other than a rifle in the cockpit and a pistol at his hip, he blanketed the area, hoping to draw a gunshot. Flying with the windows locked open so he could hear enemy ground fire or use his pistol to fire back depending on the situation, he scanned the vast area where no friendly US Army troops were but where the elusive enemy was.

FACs were loved and hated. They were loved by their fellow comrades for their uncanny ability to ferret out the bad guys so our troops could do their job pacifying hostility in Vietnam. You've heard of the old saying at wartime, "Seek and destroy." FACs were the first part of that equation. They did the seeking so that Tactical Air Support (the fighter jocks flying F-100s, F-4 Phantoms, and A-1 fighters), along with our army troops on the ground, could do the destroying.

On the other hand, VC placed bounties on every FAC's head upward of a quarter million US dollars "We were seen in their eyes as bringers of death. Our presence in the sky signified a possible attack," said Jim. Once we locked in on the enemy below, they couldn't get more than a half mile before the ground below their feet was disintegrated by missiles, bombs, and napalm (a jelly-like substance used in Vietnam that was dropped from the sky to burn off widespread areas and anything in its midst).

"On this particular day, I was headed Northeast of An Khe in my O-1 Bird Dog, traveling at a top speed of 130 miles per hour loaded down with four Willie Pete (white phosphorous) rockets," recalls Jim. White phosphorus burns fiercely and can set cloth, fuel, ammunition, and other combustibles on fire at contact. We used it to mark the location of the enemy, giving the airborne fighters a point of reference to drop their ordnance. His eyes were heavy, feeling like they were going to bleed from the sleepless night before due to a mortar attack on base camp, but they focused on the ground for any type of movement.

He hoped to get the VC to act hastily and fire at his plane, exposing themselves enough to lock in their coordinates. Something he learned since being there was to stay away from the beaten paths. Ho Chi Minh Trail was one of those paths the enemy used to provide manpower and material to the VC and North Vietnamese Army during the war—all bad guys out to kill any opposition, which included him. Ho Chi Minh Trail had been a target for AC-130 and F-100 airstrikes over the past weeks, forcing the enemy away from it into another area full of valleys, flats, and scattered hills to the far west. He was familiar with the overlay of land; if something was out of place, he'd notice. He could see an opening far ahead where smoke was rising from the base of a stretch of hills, so he pitched out a bit east at low altitude, low and slow, careful not to encounter a truck in the open. If he was shot down, he was a dead man. He didn't have enough firepower to get far by himself—the reason FACs usually died alone. Preparation was key for any fighter pilot, FACs included, which was why Jim carried a small kit on him at all times containing adrenaline injections he could administer on himself to ensure that, in a worst-case scenario, if shot down, he could evade and fight back with everything he had until falling dead with his eyes wide open.

All of a sudden, he saw something peculiar in the thick grass at the edge of a lower canopy of trees. The elephant grass there normally stood over seven feet tall. It had been beat down, signaling recent activity. It hadn't looked that way a few days ago. Jim decided to get a little closer to check it out and couldn't believe what he saw.

Sure enough, something he'd heard about but hadn't witnessed yet was the tail end of an elephant entering the edge of the thick jungle, loaded to the hilt with cargo. The VC used elephants as transports for weapons, ammunition, and other supplies used against US troops. Suddenly, he realized he'd been noticed due to the tracer fire coming at him.

Knowing he found a target, he called Tactical Air Control, "Requesting immediate fighter support."

The radio response echoed, "Roger, FAC we have your location. Fighters will be en route in minutes."

Jim, now circling over the area, noticed the enemy fire had ceased about as soon as it started. The VC lay low under the concealed jungle top, knowing they needed to move as quick as possible and hoped there were no fighters in close proximity. Little did they know, they were wrong. The radio woke with the flight leader's voice while Jim tried to draw more enemy fire from below. "FAC, this is Whiskey Lead."

Jim answered, "Whiskey Lead, this is your FAC. I've got you loud and clear. Go ahead with your lineup."

"Roger, FAC, I've got four F-100s loaded with snakes (five-hundred-pound bombs) plus fully loaded 20-millimeter cannons." He copied this information on his kneeboard with a grease pencil to reference later. Jim radioed back to Whiskey Lead, confirming there were no friendlies in the area and that he had what appeared to be a group of VC moving south through the area, carrying weapons and supplies to their forces.

He dropped to take a closer look one more time and then pulled up hard. Rolling over and then down, he fired a phosphorus rocket directly on the mark. The greenery was so bright it hurt his eyes and then he saw the curling smoke escape from the treetops from his rocket. Orbiting at ten thousand feet, Whiskey Lead said, "I've got your smoke, FAC."

Knowing what was about to happen, Jim glanced down at his map one last time to double-check his position then moved out of the way near a hillside for the strike. He then radioed, "Whiskey Lead, make your initial pass 270 as best you can, putting your bombs on my smoke, recommend pull off left. Two, three, and four, you're cleared in to continue with your bombing until all your bombs are gone. Move them around to cover the area. Again, hit my smoke. I haven't noticed any ground fire since your arrival."

Whiskey Lead left his perched position to roll in for the bomb delivery. *Boom.* He made his pass, executing delivery before pulling off to the left. Two, three, and four followed with seven-second spacing, each carefully pulling up and zigzagging out after delivery. The F-100s dropped their ordnance in perfect accordance with the smoke marker Jim strategically placed. After the last bomb was dropped, he advised the flight to hold high and dry and let him take a look. As he moved closer, he saw enemy ground fire come again. He advised the flight to keep an eye on him and then he fired another white phosphorus rocket into the ground where the enemy fire was coming from. The rocket hit the mark, and he cleared the flight in again to hit his smoke. "Whiskey flight, use your 20-mm cannons on this area." After their last pass, he advised they hold high and dry as before while he finished his bomb damage assessment (BDA), done after each strike as a matter of FAC. In this case, it was a good one— maximum damage, with numerous bodies on the ground, what appeared to be two dead elephants, and no more ground fire. "An exceptionally good strike. Thanks a lot, guys," Jim radioed.

It's been said that war is hours upon hours of boredom punctuated with moments of stark terror. Those polar opposite emotional states can take a toll on any individual. With any job, it's good to get away sometimes, and that's what Jim did next. He would leave the tropical paradise of Vietnam for a less threatening tropical setting for some rest and relaxation, but only for a week.

Jim had spent his entire tour of duty in Nam without leave. In fact, he was one of the few in the brigade who hadn't taken any time off so Archie insisted he get out of the jungle for a week, that he needed a break to put some weight back on since he had become way too thin. Jim was thankful and reached Jeanie to make plans for a trip to Hawaii in a few weeks. She replied back by letter, confirming the date, and they met there.

After a nice weeklong break, he returned to SEA with his tour nearing the end. He was anxious to get back to the war, which had done nothing but intensify. Upon returning, he would embark on one of the biggest operations of his life—Operation IRVING. The First Cavalry Division attacked at 0700 hours on the morning of 2 October 1966. Several days into the operation, Jim, Archie, and others prepared to take the Huey for a ride into the high country, near the Phu Cat Mountains. There were reports of the North Vietnamese Army transporting goods through the area, firing weapons at US helicopters, and anything else in their site. Just such a thing happened to Colonel Hyle's chopper as Jim lifted off. As soon as they raised the commander's Huey off the ground, they climbed to about twenty feet when a myriad of bullets hit the chopper's rotor, dropping them back to the ground—all 8,500 pounds—at high impact. Everyone in the Huey was checked out at the medic, and Jim's back was hurt. Still wanting to fly, not willing to let anything interfere, he grinned

SHANE ALLEN

and bared the pain in his lower back, which worsened over time. "Finally, forty-one years later, in 2007, my back was operated on, which helped, but it still bothers me," said Jim.

Later, he and Colonel Hyle climbed in a replacement Huey; their destination was a problematic area north of Qui Nhon, near an enemy village adjacent to a pristine beach area. Behind the village was a sloping hillside covered in thick vegetation leading up to an elephant grass–covered plateau, sufficient for landing the helicopter. Operation IRVING was one of three closely coordinated operations designed to destroy the enemy in the central and eastern portions of the Republic of Vietnam's Binh Dinh Province and to uproot the Viet Cong's political structure along the province's populated coastal region. Just the day before, Jim coordinated a heavy A-1 airstrike on the village of VC, who dispersed into the jungle-covered hillside. The village was now a ravaged war zone, with splintered palm trees atop piles of dead enemy attempting to flee during the attack. In the center of the riddled village, army personnel dug a large hole with a front-end loader to bury hundreds of dead enemy. The VC who managed to escape into the jungle outskirts continued to put up a fight. The brigade commander wanted to land, get out, and run in to congratulate his troops on the job they were doing. He wanted to get up close and personal as he always did. Jim tried talking him out of it, with no success. The colonel just wouldn't have it, so Jim took him close to the burning village, setting the chopper down on the flat grassy plateau where he could get out. As Hyle climbed out, two wounded soldiers were loaded on the Huey for Jim to take to the aid station about ten minutes away. Jim took the wounded soldiers to the aid station and then headed back to the check point at the top of the hill, slowing, hovering, and evaluating the landing area to make sure it was safe before pick-

192

ing up Hyle. About the time he decided it was safe to land, he was notified to hold up and check with them after some more time passed. The gunfire started up again.

"You never want to fly a big helicopter into an area where there's a gunfight if you can keep from it. The large size and slowness make it an easy target, and to take it further, you definitely don't want to set it all the way down if you can help it. It's better staying airborne to take off again if things get hot," said Jim.

He orbited the area until he heard it was okay to come back in and went for it. He hovered near the pickup point a mile from the village when he heard, "We're sending him out! We're sending him out to load now!" Jim, in the driver's seat near his copilot, saw the top half of Hyle's body in motion as he ran through the waist-high elephant grass toward the chopper. When he nearly got to the point where they would sit the chopper down, Archie dropped to the ground, disappearing into the grass. A bullet had hit him.

With the chopper several feet off the ground, Jim jumped out, telling the other pilot to hold tight. He was going to get Hyle, who still wasn't visible. He ran through the jungle grass, unable to see clearly where he was going, but he luckily stumbled upon Hyle, who was facedown. Jim rolled him over to find he was alive despite a lot of blood loss. With bullets flying, Jim grabbed him, arm over his shoulder, then started back to the Huey that quickly touched ground just in time for them to load. As the copilot lifted off again, Jim said, "Let's get to the aid station quick." With the doors wide open and he and the colonel in the back, the Huey loped. When they got there, the medics cut the colonel's shirt off to find a layer of skin peeled back from one side of his belly to the other. "It looked like someone had taken a scoop to a freshly opened gallon of ice cream," said Jim.

The aid station cleaned Hyle's graze wound and then bandaged him up in time for him and Jim to have dinner that night in the commander's tent. They did so before briefing for the day to come.

Near the end of Operation IRVING, one night near Qui Nhon, Jim had just left for the evening after briefing with the commander, and as he walked through the tent area to bed down for the night, a bullet flew in front of his nose directly through a tent beside him. "Who in the hell is playing with their gun?" he yelled. He quickly got to his tent as the fire progressed. Jim, without asking anyone, got on the radio with Tactical Air Control to call for help. While on the radio, he peeked down the hill to see a mob of VC about half a mile away charging toward the camp while firing at them. Suddenly, the galloping of First Cavalry Huey gunships echoed, followed by the chattering of the 50-caliber machine guns. The mob of VC disappeared instantly back into the jungle adjacent to the field.

Tactical Air Control confirmed, "We have a flight of eight A-1 aircraft on the way, FAC." Jim took safer cover in a nearby foxhole that he would man for the night, along with everyone else in the brigade picking a position to hold along the perimeter of the camp. As an air force officer, he was never unwilling to mix it up with the enemy on the ground by sharing responsibility with his army comrades, and he did so often. When the air strike arrived, the enemy had drawn deeper into the jungle but not far enough. The A-1's dropped a massive load of small bombs that Jim pinpointed from the edge of his foxhole. The shots stopped after the strike, but just for good measure, Jim fired his AK-47 many times into the spot they were last spotted. He did so ceaselessly until daybreak. The next morning, three dead VC were found in close proximity of camp. They were found in line with where Jim fired relentlessly through the night. This action earned him a Bronze Star.

While pressing the spreading allied coastal sweep 290 miles northeast of Saigon, Operation IRVING carried on, and Jim experienced one close call after another. He and Colonel Hyle set out to answer a report of a Sampan, a relatively flat-bottomed Chinese wooden boat filled with potential enemy VC wearing black pajamas. They flew into the suspicious area to find high ground and then touched down on a fifty-foot-high sand dune off the coastline, where they spotted the boat and waited. Jim was sitting on the skid step of the commander's Huey, making notes in his hand journal for the mission. "I remember sitting on the skid step of the Huey, and I felt sand and pebbles flicking on my pants leg. I brushed it off, not realizing I was in the gun sight of an enemy sniper. When I felt it again, it had my full attention. Soon realizing bullets were hitting the ground at my feet, very close in front of me, I knew I was being shot at by a sniper from a banana thicket about two hundred yards away," he said. "I boarded the commander's chopper with two gunners then told Colonel Hyle we would take care of the situation quickly and come back for him to leave out. The outcome was a flattened banana grove, and no more gunfire. We then picked up Archie and left." They later found it was friendlies in the Sampan, confirming no threat, so they pressed on.

The next day, Colonel Hyle told Jim to come with him in the chopper. "You got to see this," said Hyle.

Curious, Jim said, "Where we going?"

The colonel said, "You just wait and see."

They flew out an hour and a half to an area near the Mekong River, near a steep cliff, when Hyle said, "Look over on the cliff-side and tell me what you see." Jim couldn't see anything. When they got closer, he noticed movement—several men scaling down in succinct rhythm. They were Long-Range Reconnaissance Patrol (Lrrps) with the First Cavalry. "It looked like part of the cliff came alive," said Jim. LRRPs were small, heavily-armed long-range reconnaissance teams that patrolled deep in enemy-held territory.

On July 8, 1966, General William Westmoreland authorized the formation of (LRRP) units in each infantry brigade or division in Vietnam. By 1967, formal LRRP companies were organized, most having three platoons, each with five six-man teams equipped with VHF/FM AN/PRC-25 radios. LRRP training was notoriously rigorous, and team leaders were often graduates of the US Army's Fifth Special Forces Redondo School in Nha Trang, Vietnam. They were often used to set up communications towers at the top of highpoints, which is what they were doing for Hyle.

"They looked like they had been out in the muck for weeks. Their boots and socks were rotting off their feet from the dampness. They slept in the worst jungle conditions imaginable, without light or fire and unable to use noisy guns when doing this type mission," says Jim. LRRPs live among the enemy, blending in with their surroundings while on the move. Blowing their cover was not an option, something that cost them their lives in certain situations. "There were reports later that day after meeting the LRRP team. Some had been killed by tigers while trying to hold their position silently at the top of that hill while observing the enemy," said Jim.

Operation IRVING was a success in many ways. The area was heavy with enemy and also contained some 250,000 civilian residents, plus important rice-farming and salt-production areas the

United States avoided harming. To prevent noncombatant casualties, control measures were incorporated into the psychological
operations program. Some twelve million leaflets and 150 radio
broadcast hours were used during IRVING to help control the
civilians. Curfews were established, and at times, villagers were
requested to stay where they were until more specific instructions
were given. Psychological efforts were also geared to appeal to
the enemy. For example, substantial rewards were offered for sur-
rendered weapons. Simultaneously, the ARVN and Korean elements coordinated attacks in the southern portion of the battle
area so that all three schemes of maneuver would complement
one another.

By midnight of 24 October, the battle was over. The enemy
had been unable to cope with the air mobility and versatility of
the First Cavalry Division (Airmobile). Massive firepower had
decimated the enemy's forces, and its long-secure supply bases
had been destroyed. While suffering nineteen men killed themselves, the First Cavalry Division had killed 681 enemy soldiers
and captured 741. The rapid reaction of US forces allowed the
division for the first time to capture more enemy soldiers than it
killed. The success of IRVING had a lasting effect on the pacifi-
cation of Binh Dinh Province.

Nearing the end of his tour, Jim received a second Distinguished
Flying Cross, as an outcome of the operation.

Citation to Accompany the Award of
The Distinguished Flying Cross (First Oak Leaf Cluster)

To James C. Ryan

Major James C. Ryan distinguished himself by extraordi-
nary achievement while participating in aerial flight as an

Air Liaison Officer on 2 October 1966 near Xuan Binh, Phu My Province, Republic of Vietnam. On that date, Major Ryan voluntarily piloted an unarmed Command and Control UH-1D Aircraft for almost fourteen hours and participated in eight combat assault landings into an area of intense automatic weapons fire. The professional competence, aerial skill, and devotion to duty displayed by Major Ryan reflect great credit upon himself and the United States Air Force.

After the operation, Jim was trolling for fire in the O-1 near Saigon when he decided to land for a bite to eat at the officers' club at Tan Son Nhut AB. This landing would change the direction of his career altogether. When entering the officers' club, he ran into Lt. Col. Henry Jones, director of operations for the 504th Tactical Air Support Group in Bien Hoa with General Clyde McClain, who was commander of the 504th.

Jim walked in by himself and was asked to sit with them for dinner in the senior officers' dining room. They noticed his frail body and fever blister on his lip, which was cracked and bleeding. Surprised by his appearance, Jones and McClain became concerned. They couldn't let him go on with the First Cavalry, and if his wife could see how he looked at that point, they would feel responsible, so they made other plans for him. Jim was asked to come to Bien Hoa to take the role of Chief of all FACs in SEA. He headed up operational and training regulations, directives, and memorandums pertaining to flying activities of all ALOs and FACs in SEA. Jim shared his invaluable experience with all operational locations there until 12 April 1967.

Col. Archie Hyle was glad to have worked with him that year and expressed his appreciation in a written report that General Talbot, deputy director of Tactical Air Control Center, Seventh Air Force Headquarters endorsed.

Officer Effectiveness Report

7 June 66 thru 30 Nov 66

During the period that I have commanded the 1st Brigade, 1st U.S. Cavalry division (Airmobile) I know of no one who deserves more special recognition for an outstanding performance of duty than Major Ryan. He is one of those rare individuals that a Commander is seldom fortunate enough to have serve for him. His professional competence, combined with his technical knowledge and sincere desire to serve, culminated into an expertise on air support which greatly enhanced the combat effectiveness of this Brigade. His ability to anticipate the needs of the commander with an unbelievable accuracy instilled a sense of confidence within my command, and created a feeling that the brigade would never be lacking for the required air support when needed. His quick grasp of the unique aspect of our Air Assault Concept has contributed immeasurably to the Brigade's successes. If he had not been of another service I probably would have made him one of my battalion commanders. His entire attitude was one of "Can Do" and he never failed to deliver to the Brigade the required support when it was logically available. He has added so much to the success of this unit on the field of battle that I would consider his loss a near disaster.

I cannot emphasize too strongly his cooperation and the high personal and professional example he exudes. He has truly become one of the members of the 1st Team and I wish that we could claim him as our own. The Air Force is fortunate to have his service and I predict that he will go far.

Archie R Hyle, Colonel, Infantry Commanding

Additional Endorsement:

I concur with the reporting and endorsing official. Major Ryan is a most capable officer. I have been greatly impressed with the job he has done with the 1st Air Cav Div. He has represented the Air Force in an outstanding manner.

C.M. Talbott, Brig General, HQ 7th Air Force

PENTAGON

On 5 April, 1967, Jim left Bien Hoa for San Francisco and from there, to Phoenix, Arizona, to meet with his family, including his mother and father, who had stayed home with Jeanie and the boys while he was in Vietnam. He shared with the family they were moving to Fairfax, Virginia, for him to start his new job at the headquarters of the United States Air Force at the Pentagon in Washington, DC.

The family settled into a home located near the old courthouse country club, convenient for golf. Liking golf, Jim only got to play two rounds over the past year at the country club in Saigon and wanted to play more in the United States, where he didn't have to worry about being shot at during his backswing. "I can remember one day playing golf on the beautiful course in Saigon with Chester Hillhouse, a fighter pilot who flew the Bird Dog initially before going back to an F-100 squadron in Vietnam. We were playing golf when someone shot at us from a Buddhist burial site near the course, so we pulled our weapons out of our golf bags and fired back. It was a momentary distraction," said Jim. "The biggest firefight in Saigon during the war happened at the same Buddhist cemetery only a month prior."

Jim started at the Pentagon as a new major, in coat and tie, as his welcoming letter instructed. He walked through security clearance and proceeded to the operations section for the air force, which happened to be in the basement. He set up his desk in the corner, and as he sat down, he was told that he was supposed to peruse every message that came over the fax pertaining to SEA, operational events and situations that developed, plus special operations and exercises in the area. He was to pick out the ones he thought were of most importance then start developing files to present as topics of specialized briefings if appropriate. The briefing team would put together their presentations with the information.

After weeks went by, Jim was under the impression he had been forgotten about until one day, he was approached by his commander who told him there was a new rule. Two days a week, he had to start wearing a uniform, something he didn't have coming from Vietnam since he only wore fatigues there. Jim and Jeanie went to former Bolling AFB in Washington, DC, to fit for new uniforms trimmed with the proper decorations. After being sized, he went back the following couple days to pick up his new wardrobe, and that's when he found that he had obtained twenty-nine medals from his year in Vietnam, along with all the wings, jump wings, and rank to display proudly. To go with the new threads, he had new wheels. He'd bought a new car in Saigon before leaving the war which was in makeready and waiting for him to pick up in Detroit, Michigan. So he flew out that weekend to pick it up for $5,000.

That Monday, he pulled into the parking lot in a brand new *Cadillac DeVille in uniform. When he walked into the Pentagon, decorated beyond most in the building, he gained a lot of attention on his way down to the basement. His direct superior noticed him in the corner and said, "Wow, you can't sit down here with all that brass on. Come with me. We're moving you upstairs and putting you on the briefing team."

The Pentagon was four levels with a basement. The top floor was the secretary of the air force's office. Below that were four-star generals. Three-star generals were on the third floor, two-star generals on the second, and one-star generals on the first. Most of the colonels were in the basement. Jim, as a major at the Pentagon, was quickly recommended by all direct reports to be promoted to lieutenant colonel. He spent his days briefing generals from the first to the top floor, including the US Secretary of the Air Force, US Undersecretary of the Air Force, Congress, and anyone else who needed an expert opinion on SEA and the Vietnam War.

"One day, I was asked by a four-star general if all the medals I had were officially presented to me by a general officer. I didn't really even know what I had until fitting for the uniform, so the answer was no," Jim told him. For several weeks, every Wednesday, Jim was presented officially with each medal, becoming almost comical from the repetition. With more combat experience than anyone else wearing his rank, most of the time, he was the only one walking up to the podium to be honored.

He kept his flying time up by flying generals and notables in and out of Washington in the T-39. He would fly them in and out of Andrews AFB, always displaying his skills by never causing them to spill their coffee on takeoff or landing. If ever one of the generals who was also a pilot wanted to fly the aircraft, Jim obliged each one by letting them take over the controls. "They loved being back at the controls again," Jim said. "Just the same as me."

There were times when he was able to take one of the aircraft for personal purposes. His good friend BB Huffman, also recently returning from Vietnam as a FAC, was working at Tactical Air Command Headquarters in Norfolk, Virginia, and the two of them would fly into McChord AFB in the state of Washington to fish for steelhead and trout. He would fly into Florida to pick up oranges or Maine for fresh lobster. He always looked for an opportunity to keep his time up and stay current as a pilot.

His passion for flying became well-known, to the point that every Monday morning during briefing, the highest-ranking officials in the building began asking where he went this past weekend. Jim would give them a quick story, along with the weather update for their hometown, and then get into serious discussion about Vietnam, which was escalating all the time. They enjoyed his insightful conversations.

At that time, US operations had secretly crossed international borders into Laos and Cambodia, which were heavily bombed by US forces as American involvement in the war peaked in 1968. The war had gone on long enough to garner the attention of the Soviet Union, which was trying to build more nuclear arms all the time. We were trying to win the war in Vietnam while keeping close attention on the Russians, and Jim who sat many times on nuclear alert in Europe was invited to the USAF Headquarters Battle Staff war table discussions as a specialist on European affairs and operations as an action analyst. He once again impressed those around him with intelligence and presentation skills.

It was early June 1967 when Jim was working on a briefing report involving the Israeli Six-Day War that he received more good news. He was notified that he was part of the 3 percent chosen that year as a regular officer of the USAF. Officially making regular commission was a sign of respect from the air force, a badge signifying he had a future with them as opposed to a reserve that could be let go more easily.

With his vast knowledge and experience from Vietnam, he built the reputation of an expert. He took over a regular television program as a talking head for the entire Air Staff on the situation in SEA. The television broadcast reached every military base in the world. Eventually, he was briefing the highest echelons of the air force on a daily basis in a superior manner. After three years in the Pentagon, he got to know every air force general officer there by name, and they knew him as Jim. It was now 1 September 1970, and he was promoted to lieutenant colonel, a promotion that was as fast as a good fighter jet.

Officer Effectiveness Report

3 February 1971 thru 3 May 1971

Lt Col Ryan's accomplishment of tasks in an extremely sensitive and demanding assignment has been superior. His judgment was a major factor in the selection of material which he presented on a daily basis to the Secretary and Under Secretary of the Air Force, USAF Chief, Vice Chief of Staff, and the senior Air Staff as well as Deputy Chief of Staff, Plans and Operations, and Director of Operations. His research and accumulation of data concerning world-wide Air Force situations and events which were covered in the briefings enabled him to respond to queries on the spot without referral to staff agencies. He is probably one of the best informed individuals in Headquarters USAF on total Air Force Southeast Asia operations. Col Ryan personally gleaned the results of all air strikes in Cambodia, Laos and South Vietnam from hundreds of messages each day. His ability to assimilate vital facts has proven outstanding. He has the innate faculty to react quickly to emergencies and his coolness during periods of great stress added significantly to his invaluable contributions. Accuracy and thoroughness have characterized Col. Ryan's efforts despite constantly stringent time requirements. He has demonstrated a remarkable ability to plan ahead, which together with being naturally well organized, resulted in a daily product that earned him the respect and admiration of all recipients of his daily presentations.

Robert J Spence, Lt. Col
USAF Fld. Ext. Sq. (HQ COMD, USAF)

Review by Endorsing Official

I wholeheartedly concur with the comments and ratings of the reporting officer on the basis of daily observation. Lt. Col. Ryan's superior performance has been characterized by dedication and professionalism. Recommend attendance at the Air War College or comparable service school with subsequent command of flying unit. Recommend promotion to Colonel as soon as possible.

George J. Fleckenstein
Col, USAF Fld. Ext. Sq. (HQ COMD)

Additional Endorsement

Concur. Lt. Col. Ryan has an exceptionally well-organized mind and a remarkable memory. Diligent in his research, confident, composed, hardworking, completely reliable officer who daily demonstrates a superior insight into Air Force operations. Lt. Col. Ryan should be promoted to Colonel at the earliest opportunity.

Clifford W. Hargrove, Brig Gen, USAF
Operations, DCS / Plans and Operations, HQ USAF

When Jim had been told that he was going from Vietnam to his next assignment at the Pentagon, he'd fought it tooth and nail, but it turned out to be the best four years of experience he could have gotten after the Vietnam tour of duty. "I didn't want to go at first but was told I was going, so I embraced it and did the best I could," said Jim.

He was approaching four years with the Pentagon, which meant he would need to find another position soon. Jim missed the fighter business dearly and wanted to be a squadron commander of a tactical fighter squadron—something he refers to as the best job in the entire air force; the reason being you get to fly fighters while moving up. In fact, it's a very difficult job to get, with only so many squadrons to go around. Out of the roughly forty chosen annually, air force–wide, they only get to keep the job for two years before having to give it up. If you do a good job, it's almost certain you'll make full colonel rank.

The challenge for Jim, leaving the Pentagon as a lieutenant colonel, was there were so many others with the same rank looking for their next job. It was becoming tough for him to find a place to go at the end of his four years. Everyone he reached out to told him the same thing. "We would love to have you, but we have as many lieutenant colonels as we can take right now. We can't take another one, and I'm sorry, Jim."

Finding a squadron commander spot was going to be a tall order—if it was possible at all. Gen. J.C. Myers—formerly the 12th air force commander when Jim was with the 401st FBW—asked him, "What are you going to do next?"

He said, "It's funny you ask. I'm having a difficult time. Every commander I've spoken to, they tell me the same thing. 'We would like to have you, but we don't have anything since all the squadron commanders have been on the list for a year now.'"

General Myers asked him, "How would you like to spend another two years here at the Pentagon?"

Jim answered, "I appreciate you asking, but I want to be like you, sir. You were a squadron commander with great combat experience, and I want to be a squadron commander and get back to war myself."

The general said he would look into finding him a new place. Then a few days later, he called Jim in to his office and said, "Jim, tell your wife to start packing. We're sending you to Tucson, Arizona, to Davis-Monthan AFB."

It was April 1971. The 355th TFW was flying F-4 Phantoms at the time but would soon get a new single-seat, single-engine fighter that would replace the F-4.

"This will let you continue your single-engine, single-seat experience, which should be right down your alley," said General Myers.

Jim couldn't thank him enough for the opportunity. He couldn't ask for anything better. The general told him the best part about his job was helping young officers who he had full confidence in to move up.

358TH TFS

On 5 May 1971, Jim made the trip across the United States to Davis-Monthan AFB, Tucson, Arizona, while Jeanie and the boys stayed behind to sell their home in Virginia. With no base housing at the time, he moved into a housing development near a golf course called the Forty-Niner Country Club. Davis-Monthan AFB was located within the city limits and approximately five miles southeast of downtown Tucson. Just a few months later, Jim had his whole family moved into their new home in Arizona.

He had made a lot of contacts and gained great experience after the last four years at the Pentagon and was ready to get into the cockpit of a new single-seat fighter jet that just came off of the assembly line—the A7-D Corsair II. He would also find himself among more great patriots of the time. Wayman Nut was the director of operations for the 355th TFW under John Barnes, the commander of the wing. When Jim arrived, Nut and Barnes invited him to dinner, where they asked him what he wanted to do for the 355th since he technically didn't have a job yet.

"I don't think it's a secret I want to be a squadron commander," said Jim. He was told there was already the maximum number of two people on the waiting list, so maybe next year, he would have his chance. Rather, he could be the ops officer for the 40th TFS, but he would need to fully assemble it before Don Conway arrived to take it over as squadron commander. Jim knew the squadron commander position was out of reach at that point and accepted it. But over time, there would be more changes in the 355th that would seal his fate. There would also be new patriots join the wing. This included Bill Hosmer. Hosmer, known as Hoz, would arrive as vice wing commander in April 1973, someone who became a great friend to Jim and still is today.

Here's something about Hoz: Bill Hosmer, now eighty-three, flew 240 combat missions in Vietnam, as well as serving a tour as the left wing or the no. 2 flier in the famed Thunderbirds. In 1963, Hosmer flew F-105 Thunderchiefs, also known as Thuds, with the 18th Tactical Fighter Wing out of Okinawa, Japan.

The Mach 2–capable fighter-bombers were a workhorse early in the Vietnam War. The 18th TFW would regularly deploy to Korat, Thailand, where he and Jim became close. As a major, Hosmer led missions against surface-to-air missile sites, and the losses among the F-105 wings were significant. "They never had a free mission," says Jim. "When they went out, most of the time, there was some of them that wouldn't make it back."

In one picture Bill saved from that time, three of the five other men with him were shot down. One died, one was rescued, and the third spent seven and a half years as a prisoner of war. "The combat time, it was a different sort of memory. Survival and trying to do your job and bring back the people you go out with if you're a leader," Bill said.

In a second tour from 1969 to 1970, he flew F-100s with the 308th Tactical Fighter Squadron. He flew 240 combat missions—60 in the Thud, and 180 in the F-100.

Bill would finish his air force career at Davis-Monthan in 1976 as the commander of the 355th Tactical Fighter Wing. "He was one of the very best fighter pilots of the time," said Jim. "I was happy to fly with him, and it's been a great honor to have him as a friend for many years."

Again surrounded by the best, with more talent on the way, Jim was ready to get back into the cockpit of a fighter. Four years had passed since he had been in a fighter jet, so technically, he was supposed to check out in a T-33 upon getting to Davis-Monthan. Nut and Barnes were about to attend A7-D checkout school with the 333rd Training Squadron in Phoenix. When Jim initially asked if he could go and bypass the T-33 checkout—something he could do with ease—he was denied. After Nut looked into it further, he called Jim back with approval to go, which made him much happier. He had flown the T-33 so many times that it wasn't necessary. They spent weeks low-level flying, night flying, and doing range work both night and day, as well as navigation exercises to familiarize them with the advanced radar system.

The LTV A-7 Corsair II (Ling-Temco-Vought A-7 Corsair II) was a subsonic light attack aircraft. It was one of the first combat aircraft to feature a head-up display (HUD), an inertial navigation system (INS), and a turbofan engine. Radar fed a digital weapons computer that made for accurate delivery of bombs from a greater standoff distance. It far surpassed its predecessors with a plethora of cutting-edge avionics, which included data link capabilities that, among other features, provided fully "hands-off" carrier landing capability when used in conjunction with its approach power compensator (APC) or auto throttle. Other notable equipment was a projected map display located just below the radarscope. The map display was slaved to the inertial navigation system and provided a high-resolution map image of the aircraft's position superimposed over TPC/JNC charts. Moreover, when slaved to the all-axis autopilot, the inertial navigation system could fly the aircraft "hands off" to up to nine individual waypoints.

"It had a good cockpit set up because you sat high up in it. The way the wings were designed allowed you to turn like a bandit, and it held a lot of fuel. It was also computerized with a head-up display," said Jim. "I really liked the airplane."

After checking out in the A-7D, he started the role of squadron operations officer for the 40th TFS, which shared a building with the 11th Tactical Drone Squadron (TDS). He flew with the 354th TFS to keep his flight time in check while he worked on putting together the 40th. With indefatigable effort, Jim did much more than operations for the 40th TFS; he established it altogether. Lieutenant Colonel Conway was the squadron commander but wouldn't arrive from his prior assignment until much later, and everything would be in place when he did. When Jim had taken on the responsibility of putting it together, he'd started with zero assets. The first need had been men to help with administrative duties, so he'd started filtering in enlisted men to help with that. They set up desks, chairs, office supplies, and furnishings. Eventually, new pilots filtered in from the 333th Training Squadron. Jim had ferried a number of new A-7Ds in from Ling-Temco-Vought headquartered in Dallas, Texas. With pilots and planes, he had begun formulating plans for flying programs. He'd done evaluations for missions and filled out training reports as well as flight operations reports. He'd supervised briefings for aircrews, directed flight training, and addressed problems pertaining to operations. Still omnipresent, he'd done both duties of squadron commander and ops officer, now building a reputation as a pilot, supervisor, and administrator all together. By the time Conway arrived, the squadron was ready to go, and he took over with Jim as his ops officer on 1 October 1971. After eight months, things changed again.

Conway and Jim received orders to deactivate the 40th TFS and reactivate it as the 358th TFS, so they did, on 1 June 1972. Nothing changed but the name at that time, but things would soon change drastically on 13 November 1972.

Conway was promoted to assistant director of operations for the wing under Commander Nut, and Jim would fulfill his dream as squadron commander finally. He had arrived eighteen months earlier with no job and was now commander of the 358th TFS. This was the ultimate, something he had dreamed of. He chose all his men and trained them his way after they checked out in the A-7D going forward. The 358th TFS stayed busy under Jim's command by doing all the tactical air demonstrations for the 355th wing. They were also given a Panama Canal assignment as a show of force against a burgeoning Manuel Noriega. Jim took nine men from the 358th TFS including four A-7Ds to set up quarters on base in Panama.

Like everywhere else he went, he built a reputation for the 358th as the alpha squadron for keeping high standards. In large, this was from the many firepower demonstrations they performed such as Brass Key I, Exercise Brave Shield, and Coronet Organ IV. In fact, they dropped 80 percent of the entire ordinance dropped for live firepower demonstrations in the USAF during this period. They were a stellar group that called themselves the Lobos—the name Jim gave the fighter squadron. The 358th wore a patch of a wolf showing its teeth, with a lightning bolt struck behind it. The name and logo were derived from Jim's German shepherd, whose name was Lobo.

He picked the best fighter pilots and grew them into great ones. If ever someone showed signs of weakness, he would take them up personally for a dogfight to analyze their ability firsthand and correct anything that didn't fit the bill. If they responded the right way, they got better. If they didn't, he moved them out. Jim didn't tolerate scuttlebutts among his men; he squashed it the minute he heard of a problem. He always praised his men in public and criticized them in private. Having the best squadron in the air force was his standard, and he showed his guys how to do it.

Officer Effectiveness Report

22 June 73 thru 20 December 73

Review by Endorsing Official

This man is a winner. Lt. Col. Ryan is one of the finest tactical fighter squadron commanders I have ever known. He is a totally professional fighter pilot and leader of men. He is Wing Commander material. He is fully qualified for immediate promotion and he is capable of handling much greater responsibilities.

Fred A. Haeffner, Colonel
Commander, 355TFW (TAC)
Davis-Monthan AFB, AZ

It didn't take long for the 358th to reach combat-ready status, something they put to good use on December 1973 by deploying to the Korat Royal Thai AFB for six months. This was something they worked hard for, and they were excited to go.

They would attach to the 354th Tactical Fighter Wing out of Myrtle Beach and split into rear and advanced echelons. The 353th and advanced 355th TFSs deployed (seventy-two) A-7Ds to Korat Royal Thai AFB, Thailand. This was the first combat deployment of the A-7D into Southeast Asia. This operation was known as Constant Guard VI.

From Korat, the 354th interdicted lines of communications to halt the flow of North Vietnamese supplies to enemy units in South Vietnam, provided close air support to ground troops, and escorted surface ship convoys up the Mekong River to Phnom Penh, Cambodia. In November 1972, the 354th took over the combat search and rescue role formerly assigned to the A-1 "Sandy" aircraft, and during the Linebacker II campaign, it assisted in twenty-two rescues of downed airmen while simultaneously flying over four thousand combat sorties. The wing earned the Presidential Unit Citation for its Vietnam War service from September 1972 through January 1973.

In March 1973, A-7D aircraft drawn from the deployed Myrtle Beach squadrons were formed into the 3rd Tactical Fighter Squadron and permanently assigned to the host 388th TFW at Korat.

In addition to its Myrtle Beach squadrons, the advanced 354th TFW had the following temporary A-7D squadrons attached while at Korat: They were the 354th TFS out of Davis-Monthan, the 74th TFS out of England AFB, and the 358th out of Davis-Monthan, which was Jim's. He and the 358th rotated in on 28 December 1973. They stayed through 15 May 1974, flying combat missions in support of the Cambodian government, and while they were there, something bittersweet happened. Jim had fulfilled his time as commander of the 358th TFS and turned over the position in May 1974 before they rotated back to Davis-Monthan. He made full colonel and stayed in Vietnam with two guys he started with as green 16.

His old friends were in position to keep Jim's spirits up by keeping him back in the war for more than a short stint. Roger Sprague was on his way to become director of operations for the 388th TFW, and Deacon Russell was commander. They asked

Jim to stay as assistant DO for the 388th TFW, something he was happy to do, especially since he started with Sprague and Russell back in 1954 at Alexandria AFB. By the time Jim arrived in Korat in 1973, things started winding down. There were flying exercises primarily to remain combat-ready during the transition from war to peace, but most of the combat action was over, or so it appeared. However, there was one more operation at the very end—the last fight in the Vietnam War.

In May 1975, A-7Ds were used in the SS MAYAGUEZ operation, the last combat action of the United States in Southeast Asia. Jim was a part of the SS MAYAGUEZ operation with the 3rd TFS, flying a mission in the A7-D. The Mayaguez incident, which took place between the Khmer Rouge and the United States from May 12–15, 1975, was the last official battle of the Vietnam War. The names of the Americans killed, as well as those of three US Marines who were left behind on the island of Koh Tang after the battle and who were subsequently executed by the Khmer Rouge, are the last names on the Vietnam Veterans Memorial.

America's involvement in the Vietnam War started December 1956 and speculatively ended with the fall of Saigon on 30 April 1975. Jim was one of the last USAF colonels to leave mid-May of 1975. His next job would be chief of safety for Twelfth Air Force Tactical Air Command Headquarters at Bergstrom AFB, southeast of downtown Austin, Texas.

The 358th TFS was inactivated in a ceremony held at Davis-Monthan AFB on Friday, 21 February 2014, as part of the USAF's Total Force Initiative (TFI) policy. The squadron facilities and aircraft were assumed by the Air Force Reserve's 47th Fighter Squadron, which had inactivated in late 2013 at Barksdale AFB, Louisiana, and relocated to Davis-Monthan in order to be reactivated as an AFRC A-10 Formal Training Unit (FTU) on March 2014. The A-10 could soon be retired to the boneyard. On 24 February 2014, Secretary of Defense Chuck Hagel introduced a plan which would retire the A-10 in order to provide funding for the F-35A. The plan emphasizes capability over capacity; the multirole F-35 and most other combat aircraft can carry precision-guided munitions, so the single-mission A-10 would be divested in order to speed up F-35 production.

MOVING UP

With Jim's last tour in Vietnam at an end, Twelfth Air Force Headquarters needed him to head up a major safety initiative for every air force base west of the Mississippi River. His diverse background and resume loaded with great accolades made him a perfect fit for chief of safety.

He would report to Lt. Gen. James D. Hughes, commander of Twelfth Air Force Headquarters, who would continue to grow Jim's resume in various ways, including a college degree, which he needed in order to get the next promotion to general, something that was being discussed. When he arrived at Bergstrom AFB, he had missed the enrollment deadline, something General Hughes was able to extend in order to put him on the path of a bachelor's degree. He applied for Bootstrap, the education opportunity program which accounted for accumulated hours, experience, track record, and endorsements, which was not a problem. Jim was able to test out of many courses (CLEP), which allowed him to expedite the process of acquiring his bachelor of science degree in general studies at the American Technological University in Killeen, Texas, with As and Bs. While he did his job as chief of safety, he went to college full time.

He also worked closely with another air force colonel who needed positive influence and understanding—a Vietnam POW.

Something you may not realize in relation to Vietnam prisoners of war, they were granted due promotion while being in the Hanoi Hilton—the worst imaginable prison for captives. Severely abused and tortured, some for many years, they went in as young men with low rank and came out high rank. Stifled from incarceration, they didn't have the ability to gain more experience, education, or know-how. They were just stuck, but their promotions progressed.

The United States addressed this appropriately with some finesse by giving them deserving rank; after all, they were on duty. The assistant chief of safety at Twelfth Air Force Headquarters who worked with Jim was a newly promoted colonel whose name was Jack Van Loan.

Van Loan was a POW for seven years. He kept himself mentally stable by rehearsing his golf game over and over in his head. He would play many different courses, some of the best in the United States over and over again. From the tee box on number 1 to the back 9 holes, he drove long, made it on the green in one or two, and one putted many times. Some days he played better than others, weather permitting. He even traded his golf clubs for a newer improved set when needed. Every aspect of the game, he lived day in and day out while being beaten, starved, and confined.

When Jack was set free and returned to the United States, he found a golf course right away and shot par.

Jim was chief of safety and Jack was assistant chief of safety. The job was a big responsibility, which was lacking at the time Jim took the helm. As chief of safety, a principal staff officer, he was responsible for safety programs in eight active bases covering ground, munitions, and air operations, which involve nine different fighter or recce weapons systems. He worked directly with the Twelfth Air Force commander, wing commanders, and major command staff agencies. Jim's assistant, Jack, was a great man but had many things to do in order to overcome the nightmare he lived as a POW, leaving greater responsibility on Jim. "The prisoners of war in Vietnam or any war had a very tough time, and they deserve all the help they need," said Jim.

One of the memorable projects Jim took on as chief of safety involved one of his bases with a growing problem. One particular base, Cannon AFB in Clovis, New Mexico, had an issue with car accidents on the rise; many were alcohol-related. "I knew that the only way I would be able to turn this serious problem around was get all the enlisted guys and officers' attention while earning their respect. Setting new policies and procedures wouldn't do it, cracking down on the base police wouldn't help either," said Jim.

He decided to bring in the world's most famous racecar driver, someone that everybody would be drawn to. He came up with Richard Petty, who was flattered to help out. It didn't take long for the word to get out, and they had great attendance for what was technically an awareness campaign for reckless driving. Everyone came out and listened to Petty, who gave some great advice. "Don't be careless and, more importantly, don't be stupid," he said. "This is not a race. The cars you are driving are not built for a high-speed race, and I wouldn't race one of your cars. No way, no how! It's a wonder more of you haven't died. I've been given the accident reports, the number of traffic citations, and all the information. I surely wouldn't drive any car if I had a drink. That's asking for it." It was the perfect example of kicking those who needed reprimand in the ass while patting them on the back at the same time. Accident reports dropped after that evening.

Another issue that was addressed—Twelfth Air Force–wide—involved what was sighted as foreign object damage (FOD) meaning a foreign object causing damage to an aircraft in flight or near the runway. If a small bolt, bird, or any other small object ricocheted into the intake of a fighter jet, it could cause major damage or engine failure leading to an accident.

Jim put good emphasis on FOD, walking the runways and ramps regularly. He also implemented the use of stationary propane-powered crow guns that fired loud blasts to scare birds from specific areas. He approached his job with zest, making a difference that saved lives. With such big responsibility, he still managed to find some opportunity to fly.

Jim got to fly a new jet while he was chief of safety traveling to Nellis AFB for a routine procedure. When he was there, the wing commander asked him if he would like to fly the new F-111. He quickly said, "Let's do it." Each time he went back, he flew it. The F-111 pioneered several technologies for production aircraft, including variable-sweep wings, afterburning turbofan engines, and automated terrain-following radar for low-level, high-speed flight. Its design influenced later variable-sweep wing aircraft, and some of its advanced features have since become commonplace. The F-111 suffered a variety of problems during initial development, and several of its intended roles failed to materialize. "It wasn't a plane that you hear anyone brag much about flying, but it was still flying," said Jim.

He was in the process of taking final exams his last semester in college when he received an unnerving call. His father's health was declining, and he was in the hospital. Jim had two more tests to take but worked it out so that he could go and see his father. "When I walked into the room, he was in severe pain and on strong medication. He had been diagnosed with diverticulitis and was going to have to be operated on. When I stepped next to his bed, he looked up at me and pinched at my cheek, telling me to get the beard off my face. He said, "What are you doing with that scruff on your face? Get that off now." Jim didn't have a beard; he was as clean-shaven as always. This concerned Jim beyond comfort. His father had been his best friend, and that stemmed from way back. He was different now. His health wasn't good.

When getting back to Austin, Jim got his degree in August of 1976. He had spent a year in Texas, so he also got a new assignment. It was a bigger job than he had done to date—base commander of Cannon AFB in Clovis, New Mexico. It was the same base he had developed a relationship with when he resolved their driving challenges, and they were happy to see him come. Not only did Jeanie and the boys move out with Jim, he brought his parents with him too so he could make sure his dad got proper and timely medical attention.

As a base commander, you are responsible for the entire base—the people and infrastructure, including roads, water and sewer, chapel programs, base security, family housing, base housekeeping, and recreational outlets. Even the dogs, cats, and children were included. There were 5,500 people on base made up of civilians and military. The job is equivalent to that of a city manager. Every complaint or base issue, if severe enough, would end up on Jim's desk. He was now responsible for an entire air force base and supporting the Twenty-Seventh Tactical Fighter Wing, yet at this point in his career, he rarely got to fly a fighter plane himself. Rather, he flew a desk and a fast one. He missed the fighters and the lifestyle of a fighter pilot. His job, like all executive positions, became more and more administrative in nature, not to mention political. Jim made a network of connections with the civilian world—from the mayor to the chamber of commerce, he represented the base in the communities around him. Coordinating investigations on aircraft accidents was as close as he got to a fighter jet at this point—those that were annihilated on the ground. There were a couple of F-111 crashes involving the 27th Tactical Fighter Wing, which fell back on Jim to sort out.

As any good leader does, Jim always made a point to surround himself with the best people. He was closely involved with a group of fifty, who sat on a military affairs committee and got things done for him. They helped him manage local issues as well as nationally. They lobbied in Washington DC for the purposes of the base. They were doctors, lawyers, business owners, dignitaries, and people he had built great relationships with. Jim worked well with them, and they accomplished a great deal for Cannon AFB together. The committee showed great esprit de corps (unity). With Jim's help, they got a great deal done, including the construction of a new childcare center, a base recreation center, and an officers' open mess—their club. Jim garnered great respect from every enlisted person, officer, and civilian on the base. The commander of the Fighter Wing, Col. Thomas Hickey, had the utmost respect for Jim because of his great leadership ability. Even though Jim wasn't directly involved with the Fighter Wing, he was their support system. His sheer presence made the wing better. From the least experienced pilot up to the wing commander—they all admired him and gained from him being there.

They would be sad to see him go. Jim decided he would retire on 1 July 1978. Just before his announcement, Cannon AFB was awarded the most improved in appearance within the Twelfth Air Force. Jim was referred to by Twelfth Air Force Commander Hughes as the best colonel in the Twelfth Air Force and quite possibly the entire Tactical Air Command. One might ask, why didn't he stay to make the highest rank in the military? The answer is easy. "When I no longer had a seat in the cockpit, I didn't want to do it anymore," says Jim.

He had made so many friends in Clovis that he stayed there with his family for the next two years, playing golf and catching up on quality time with family. The Ryans had gotten to see all parts of the United States, but they hadn't saw Oklahoma in a while. By this time, his parents had already moved back there. The time had come for them to follow suit. Jim started the life of an adventurer in eastern Oklahoma as a child. It would only be fitting to get back to his roots there and build a house on Broken Bow Lake, so they did. He flew planes privately for business until 2003, worked as a fishing guide on the lake, contracted as a scuba diver, helping tourists who dropped their keys or wallet in the water at the marina, and played golf, of course. He owned and operated a country and western club with his son, Tony. His parents were an hour away in Red Oak, near Lodi, where Jim was born. He and his father did a great deal of fishing together until Ernest passed away from stomach cancer in 1988. In his last hours, he gave Jim a hundred-dollar bill; he was always trying to give him money. Jim tried giving it back, but Ernest would never take it. To this day, Jim still has the hundred in his wallet. He's carried it around for over a quarter century.

He lost his mother in 1995 to natural causes. Both Ernest and Faye are buried in Broken Bow, Oklahoma, and he talks of them often.

After finishing the manuscript for this book, something tragic happened the day after Easter, April 21, 2014. Jim and Jeanie were in a car accident in Highland Village, Texas, where Jim survived with a broken leg, bumps, and bruises. Jeanie didn't survive. Their sixtieth wedding anniversary was a month away. She was laid to rest at the Dallas-Fort Worth National Cemetery on April 30, 2014.

Today, Jim resides in Lantana, Texas, where he misses his wife dearly but continues spending time with both sons and their families in Texas also. He and Jeanie have eight grandchildren, including triplets who are the youngest. The number of great-grandchildren is growing.

Jim and Jeanie's oldest son, Jim Lee, spent over twenty-five years with the US Army including the First Cavalry's First Brigade. Bilingual, he learned to speak fluent Russian while in the military and now works for the National Security Administration. He still remembers when his dad went to William Tell and brought him a parachute home as a souvenir. "Now when I look back, especially after having spent twenty-two years in the army myself, I better understand the commitment needed by the military and how much you must give up, living that life. I also understand that my father did the absolute best he could to balance his commitment to his family and his career. The demand on the life of a true patriot is never easy," said Jim Lee.

Younger Tony didn't spend time in the military but followed his entrepreneurial spirit after attending college. He is a successful business owner and professional bow fisherman, who established the making of a cable television series revolving around the sport. At age six, he insisted his schoolteacher call him Jim Tony Ryan in the classroom because he changed his first name to Jim like his dad and brother. He did this when his dad was deep into his first tour of the Vietnam War. Tony is the vice president of communications for the HALO for Freedom Warrior Foundation and a contributor to helping wounded soldiers. He is an avid skydiver, part of an elite group within the HALO for Freedom Foundation that jumps into various special events while flying a giant US flag all the way down to promote patriotism. "My father is my hero," says Tony.

CLOSE

Col. Jim Ryan proved without a shadow of a doubt that he had plenty of ability to reach the highest levels of the air force, but making high rank wasn't why he'd gone in. More rank brought more administrative work accompanied by politics, and Jim enjoyed neither. Fighter planes were now scenery from his office window, something he had to witness day in and out. He'd hitchhiked to the recruiting station with one thing on his mind—to fly fighters. It was something he did at the highest level despite all odds. Taken under the wing of the greatest American flying aces of all time, as well as some of the most courageous army commanders who ever tromped a muddy boot in Vietnam, he'd been trained by the best.

The greatest generation, coined by Tom Brokaw, describes a generation who grew up in the United States during the deprivation of the Great Depression and then went on to fight in World War II, as well as those whose productivity within the war's home front made a decisive material contribution to the war effort.

People are born with instinct; each and every one of us has it, but some live an entire life without using it. The greatest generation depended on their instinct for survival. There was no buffer between them and complete failure. When protected by someone or something—for instance, the government—you never have to dig deep enough to discover your true ability. It remains untapped. It's truly a sad reality that weakens our nation. Generations since have disappointed by skirting traditional values, holding their hands out all the way with a sense of entitlement. This is not the way Col. Jim Ryan lives his life.

As Jim put it, "The fearless attitude is an attitude that not enough of the American people today know enough about."

Jim and I met in a very peculiar way. I owned a local newspaper group in North Texas, something I'd run for a decade before selling. We published a column in our newspapers written by Randy Haberman of Flower Mound, Texas. The title was "War", and the underlying point was why America hadn't won a war since WWII. In short, the answer includes the rules of engagement, brought on by The Hague and Geneva Conventions, covering the rights of people in war and warfare proper or the use of weapons in war. "No war is won until you have the surrender of the opposing government, citizens, and their military. It has to be total and complete capitulation," said Jim. In order to gain total surrender, lives would inevitably be lost on both sides. That was war. It's hard to win a war while worrying if you're fighting fair or treating a violent and dangerous prisoner fairly. Certain things are obvious—for instance, killing the helpless and harmless; that's a matter of morals. But court-martials for war crimes that save American lives are another thing. Somewhat recently, three Navy SEALs who'd pulled off the perfect mission—bringing a terrorist leader to justice without firing a shot—were court-martialed because of a scratch recognized on the prisoner's face the day after. This is plain ludicrous, particularly if the prisoner inflicted pain on himself, knowing how to play off of America's weakness of being overly fair.

America still hasn't won a war since WWII and hasn't named a five-star general since. It was a different time after the Second World War, truly a great time for America. It was a time when cars were manufactured by American sweat, oil came from Texas, and stores were closed on Sunday to slow things down a bit. Children placed their small hands over their big hearts to say the Pledge of Allegiance to the flag before school then prayed on their knees, thankful for the freedom that their grandfathers and fathers fought for, and if a tear rolled down their cheek, it wasn't viewed as weakness but pride.

It was a time when an ambitious high school graduate could go to the movies with his girlfriend and be inspired to the point he would hitchhike to the air force recruiting office thirty miles away, signing up to find himself an American fighter pilot and decorated war hero nearly sixty-five years later. It was a time when an American could find passage to realizing their dreams under the wing of a patriot.

BIBLIOGRAPHY

Acheson, Dean. *Present at the Creation: My Years in the State Department.* 1st ed. New York: Norton, 1969.

Air Cav: History of the 1st Cavalry Division in Vietnam 1965–1969. Nashville: Turner Pub. Co., 2011.

Air Force Magazine. "Records, Trophies, Competitions." http://www.airforcemag.com/magazinearchive/magazine%20documents/1996/may%201996/0596records.pdf (accessed May 8, 2014).

Ashcroft, Dr. Bruce. "We Wanted Wings." http://www.aetc.af.mil/shared/media/document/AFD-061109-026.pdf (accessed May 8, 2014).

Blesse, F. C. "Preface." In No guts, no glory! Nellis AFB: Nev., 1955.

Bowman, Martin W. Lockheed F-104 Starfighter, Ramsbury, Marlborough, Wiltshire. UK: Crowood Press Ltd., 2000.

Coram, Robert. *Boyd: The Fighter Pilot Who Changed the Art of War.* Boston: Little, Brown, 2002.

Craven, Wesley Frank. The Army Air Forces in World War II. Washington, DC: Office of Air Force History, 1983.

Donald, David, ed. Century Jets. Norwalk, Connecticut: AIRtime Publishing, 2003.

Dunnigan, James F. and Albert A. Nofi. Dirty Little Secrets of the Vietnam War. New York: Thomas Dunne Books, 1999.

1st Air Cavalry Division: Memoirs of the First Team, Vietnam, August 1965–December 1969. Sl: 1st Air Cavalry Division, 1970.

Kristensen, Hans M. U.S. Nuclear Weapons in Europe. New York: Natural Resources Defenses Council, 2005.

Lester, Gary Robert. *Mosquitoes to Wolves: The Evolution of the Airborne Forward Air Controller.* Maxwell Air Force Base, Alaska: Air University Press, 1997.

McEwen, Scott and Richard Miniter. *Eyes on Target: Inside Stories from the Brotherhood of the U.S. Navy SEALs, Including SEAL Heroism During the 9/11 Attack on Benghazi.* Unabridged ed. Hachette Book Group, 2014.

The McChord Air Museum Foundation. "The Will Tell Weapons Meet." McChord Air Museum Homepage. www.mcchordairmuseum.org (accessed May 8, 2014).

Michel, Marshall Louis. *The Revolt of the Majors: How the Air Force Changed after Vietnam.* Auburn: Auburn University, 2006.

Miner, Craig. "James Jabara: Hero." http://www.wingsoverkansas.com/?s=James+Jabara (accessed May 8, 2014).

Peers, William R. and Dean Brelis. *Behind the Burma Road, the Story of America's Most Successful Guerrilla Force.* 1st ed. Boston: Little, Brown, 1963.

Staff, Officer Effectiveness Reports, Washington DC: United States Air Force, Ref. James C. Ryan, 1952–1978.

Walton, Andrew R. *The History of the Airborne Forward Air Controller in Vietnam.* Oxford, Mississippi: University of Mississippi, 1993.

Robert Coram, *Boyd: The Fighter Pilot Who Changed the Art of War* New York: Little, Brown, 2002

Staff, DEFCON DEFense CONdition:Federation of American Scientists. http://fas.org/nuke/guide/usa/c3i/defcon.htm